LIFE IS A SERIES OF UNEXPECTED INTERRUPTIONS

THE UNTOLD REAL-LIFE STORY OF HOW ONE BAD DECISION DESTROYED A MULTIMILLIONAIRE'S LIFE & HIS ROAD BACK TO GOD, FAITH, AND LOVE

CLARK EAST

Life is a Series of Unexpected Interruptions
2nd Edition
Copyright © 2022, 2020 Clark East

All Rights Reserved. No part of this publication may be reproduced, distributed, or transmitted in any form or by any means, including photocopying, recording, or other electronic or mechanical methods, without the prior written permission of the publisher, except in the case of brief quotations embodied in critical reviews and certain other noncommercial uses permitted by copyright law.

Elite Online Publishing is committed to publishing works of quality and integrity. In that spirit, we are proud to offer this book to our readers; however, the story, the experiences, and the words are the author's alone. The conversations in the book all come from the author's recollections, not word-for-word transcripts. All of the events in this memoir are true to the best of the author's memory. The author, in no way, represents any company, corporation, or brand mentioned herein. The views expressed in this memoir are solely those of the author.

Clark East
Sugar Land, TX
ClarkEastAuthor.com

In Association with:
Elite Online Publishing
63 East 11400 South Suite #230
Sandy, UT 84070
EliteOnlinePublishing.com

Printed in the United States of America

ISBN - 979-8672028156 (Amazon)
ISBN - 978-1513660486 (Paperback)
ISBN - 978-1513660622 (Hardback)

Acknowledgements

There are so many people to thank who stood by me and never left me. They did not judge me and believed in me, even when I stopped believing in myself.

To my mother, Bonnie East, who is my biggest supporter, showing me unconditional love. To my three remarkable and beautiful children: Jamie, Jonathan, and Brendan. Thank you for loving me even when it was difficult to accept and understand what my poor choices put each of you through. Your love is what kept me going. To my four grandchildren: Jack, Taylor, Aiden, and Emily, for keeping me grounded in honesty, humility, gratitude, and always inspiring me to be better. To my sister, Sue, and my brother-in-law, Byron Novosad, my constant rocks, foundation, and support to come home to. To my true friends who stuck with me throughout my life and journey. Prentiss Smith, my brother from another mother, best friends for 40 years. To Bill Watson, who said, "God never left you, I never left you, you left God, and you left me." Thank you, Bill, for your moral compass and constant friendship of 25 years. To Sonny Molloy, who never stopped believing in me and after 25 years of friendship, was waiting for me to return from the prison camp to help me restart my development business.

I thank each of you from the bottom of my heart. I never realized what unconditional love and friendship really meant until I lived through this journey of mine. God, Faith, and Love are truly the trinity of life.

To Patty Tucker Rice, who showed me I can love again and what Unconditional Love is.

Thank you all for reminding me what is important and for loving me when I could not love myself. And to my former wife, Elaine Switzer, who gave me the title to this book more than 20 years ago. Little did we know the real meaning of *Life is a Series of Unexpected Interruptions*.

To Ed Catanzaro and Owen Prestridge for your love and support and your many camp visits.

To my older brother Blaine in working with me from the start and my younger brother Dave who has always been there for me through thick and thin. After all three of my heart attacks, Dave was by my bedside every time I woke up.

You are fearless.

For you keep going after your dreams,

long after others would quit.

But, you're not like others.

If you're struggling,

it means you're trying.

It means you're not giving up.

It means this dream matters.

And, the Universe knows this.

Don't quit right before

your miracle happens.

Dedication

To my three children, Jamie East Billig, Jonathan Clark East, and Brendan Scott East. You are my whole world.

Table of Contents

Acknowledgements i

Dedication v

Foreword ix

Introduction 1

    LIFE IS A SERIES OF UNEXPECTED INTERRUPTIONS

Chapter 1 7

    PLANTED A SEED

Chapter 2 17

    PUMPED UP COLLEGE DAYS

Chapter 3 27

    MARRIAGE AND CAREER CHANGE

Chapter 4 51

    RISE AND FALL OF THE SAVINGS AND LOAN (S&L)

Chapter 5 61

    MOVING ON

Chapter 6 77

    INTERRUPTED

Chapter 7 79

    FLORIDA SPORTS HALL OF FAME

Chapter 8 91

    LOOKING INWARD — UPWARD

Chapter 9 97

    RESIDENTIAL DRUG ABUSE PROGRAM (RDAP)

Chapter 10.. 103

    TURNING POINT

Chapter 11.. 109

    THREE RIVERS

About the Author 125

Foreword

A journey from a fortunate middle-class family of privilege, and wealthy multimillionaire developer lifestyle, to the soul-crushing prison life that taught me what truly is important in life — *love*. If you want to save yourself from reading this whole book, there's your answer. *Love*. It's a very simple word and few words could speak volumes about ourselves and those around us. Love truly makes the world go round. It is what saves us from ourselves. Love redeems us from our deepest darkest despair. It is our light when we are lost in the woods. Love does not let our mistakes define us. Love helps us learn from our mistakes and changes our direction, guiding us to a newer, better, and brighter tomorrow. Love defines us.

My own life that has been full of unexpected interruptions, has taught me patience, humility, and gratitude. However, the most important lesson for me is that all my poor choices in the past do *not* define who I am today. Those choices were merely made out of fear. Baseless, faceless, false fear playing out in my mind. This fear led me to the emotional, irrational, and disastrous decisions that ultimately tore apart everything that I had built for myself and my family, everything in life that was worth living for, or so I thought.

This fear was strong enough to even stop me from putting an end to the fear, that's how powerful fear had become in my life. It controlled my emotions, actions, and my will to stand up to myself and face reality. Some of the world's greatest cowards are staring back at you through the mirror.

Don't look away, that's what they want you to do. Stand up to them.

I held onto my fear like some people would keep a dirty little family secret, or rather my fear kept me like a servant. It was certainly something that I was experiencing in real-time, where there was a financial burden or relationship conflict. I was making decisions out of fear, and I kept making one poor choice after another because I did not want to face the coward in the mirror. He was an ugly bully, and I couldn't look him in the eye.

My fear had a few friends, stubborn pride was one of his closest allies. It was vanity that kept me from owning up to the reality that sometimes prevented me from making the best decisions in the moment. It was vanity that convinced me that I could hide my mistakes and keep my reputation as a dealmaker. Vanity was a real SOB to deal with every night.

As I look back now, if I had faced that fear and displaced my vanity, I would have been alright. I would have recovered, and my life would have carried on to another project, another deal. My problems would not have been half as difficult as the consequences were for my actions that brought me to my knees.

If only I had remembered what love was. Sadly, I had forgotten all about it. I forgot that love brought me into this world. Love carried me through school, into my first deal, and onto my next.

As you read about my journey, my unexpected interruptions, I want you to know that no matter your mistakes nor what seems to be failures, know that these are just little interruptions that may lead you to where you need to be. You need not fear them nor any other obstacle in life. You are, however, encouraged to learn and grow.

A friend of mine once told me, "Nothing succeeds in life more than failure." It never made more sense to me than when I was almost finished writing my book. If it weren't for all these failures, I wouldn't have become the success that I am today.

I hope you enjoy my journey and pass it along if you find something worth talking about.

Warm regards, Clark East
Director of Lost Accounts
Accounts Payable-Forward

> *"Do not go where the path may lead, go instead where there is no path and leave a trail."*
> *—Ralph Waldo Emerson*

Introduction

LIFE IS A SERIES OF UNEXPECTED INTERRUPTIONS

Have a seat and take a deep breath, then ask yourself, "What unexpected interruption propelled you to be the person you are today?"

I'll bet you can think of hundreds of little decisions that forced your course correction to be in the place you are in now. Profession choices, life events, and life decisions can lead us along paths down which we never thought we would walk. What enables a person to be the person they were meant to be — the person God meant you to be? What unexpected interruption changed your life?

Have you ever experienced a squall? It's a sudden, sharp increase in wind speed lasting minutes, contrary to a wind gust lasting a few seconds. They usually are associated with active weather, such as rain showers, thunderstorms, or heavy snow. You could be sitting in your boat on a cool afternoon fishing for dinner, reaching for your sack lunch, and the next thing you know, you're spitting out salt water.

My story begins early, and each interruption not only changed my life, but the journey that led me to write this book is the most unexpected journey of a lifetime. It's not just one life interruption that we experience. Most of us can agree that life is full of unexpected interruptions that lead you to a path of destruction and/or healing. You can choose to find purpose, renewal, or discovery. Instead of accepting a terrible ending, you can choose to find a new beginning. After all, life is an open prism of ends and beginnings. You will experience chapters in life that are completely unexpected, but you'll also find bountiful blessings if you allow yourself to breathe, listen, and absorb those precious moments right in front of you. Open your eyes. You'll see the purpose of your journey.

Clark at the start of his career in 1981

INTRODUCTION

Even when it seems like there is no purpose, no light at the end of the tunnel, I can promise that these are the moments of learning and a time for growth. I hope by sharing this story that you will understand what I mean and see the same aspects of growth and opportunities in your own life. It's when we look back that we see how we arrived where we are.

> *"Every single thing that has ever happened in your life is preparing you for something that is meant to come."*
> *— Author Unknown*

> "Giant oak trees... have deep root systems that can extend two-and-one-half times their height. Such trees rarely are blown down regardless of how violent the storms may be."
> —Joseph B. Wirthlin

INTRODUCTION

*Every story has a
beginning and an end.*

This one is mine.

> "The seeds of resilience are planted in the way we process the negative events in our lives."
>
> — Sheryl Sandberg

Chapter 1
PLANTED A SEED

At around 10 years old, while in the fifth grade, I realized something about myself that would continually define the choices I made through to adulthood. It was an accident or some divine moment that made me stop and decide what type of person I would grow up to be. I wanted to be better than my father.

Make no mistake, I loved my dad. I thought the world of him. He was my hero growing up and all through my life. But at that one tender moment as a fifth grader, something seemed more important to me than anything else in the world. My vanity stepped on me for the first time and I didn't recognize it. My vanity told me that I was worth more and that I could do better than that man standing in front of me, my own dad. He stood 5' 10" and was built like a Sherman tank. He was no-nonsense, no BS, business slacks, and short-sleeved shirt — never jeans and sneakers — Salem smoking, larger than life itself — *Dad*.

Hell, he could have been Ronald Reagan's twin brother. They called him "Big Daddy" because of his take no prisoners, hold no quarter, command of a job site. "My way or the highway," said Big Daddy East. "Son, you're going to wind up an S.O.B. in the end, you might as well be an S.O.B at the beginning and set everyone's expectations."

My dad, Douglas East, was from Lake Charles, Louisiana. He was a building contractor, real estate broker, floor covering contractor (sales and installation), and a furniture salesman.

My dad was the hardest-working person I have ever known. He found success as a self-made, self-taught entrepreneur and contractor developer. He remodeled houses, apartments, hotels, and commercial buildings. My dad even owned many of the buildings he remodeled. He was a second-generation developer as well since his dad, Thomas Sadler East, built the Oil Center in Lafayette, Louisiana.

My brother and I would work with my dad on weekends. I was one of four children in my family of three boys and one girl. My oldest brother, Blaine, is two years older than me, and my sister, Sue, is in the middle of the two of us. Our little brother, Dave, is four years younger than I am. There's something about being the middle child that makes you want to try harder than the others to be noticed or appreciated. Blaine was the oldest and he was recognized as the oldest. Sue was the only girl, so you know she was the favorite girl in the family, and David was the youngest, so the baby, and got all the extra attention, leaving me, the middle child, left out of the sack race. They say that middle children make out to be great negotiators, and I wasn't going to let down that stereotype for all the tea in China. I was determined to make something of myself and earn my dad's respect.

Blaine joined me working weekends with Dad on job sites. We were sometimes paid 50 cents to sweep floors and pick up trash, load and unload trucks, stack boxes of tile, or just watch Dad's employees or subcontractors go about their business. We made enough money for the day and spent it all at the Ben Franklin Five & Dime store on our way home every evening.

My moment of clarity happened while working a commercial project in Lafayette, Louisiana. It is where my story started, and my dream began. As we cleaned up a job site as usual, a big, long, black Cadillac crept onto the job site and parked in front of my father. My brother and I just stood there and watched with anticipation. We expected to see a bank president, some important person from the mayor's office, or maybe even the governor step out of the car. It was Maurice Heymann, the developer and owner of that property to give my dad a few last-minute instructions and changes to the plan.

Mr. Heymann was one of the most influential Jews in Lafayette history and a very wealthy man, not an all-important politician or power broker. He was a straightforward business owner who worked like everyone else to earn a living, he was just a little smarter than most. He was in his early 60s, with gray hair, and built about the same as my dad. He usually wore khaki pants with a white shirt. Dad used to say that he had, "…more money than Carter had liver pills."

I watched my father shake his head a few times and nod, "Yes, sir," "No, sir." Although that was a common language from my dad and all of us, there was something about the tone in my dad's voice. Mr. Heyman looked bigger than my dad, and most of all — his car was a statement of power and control! The long black Cadillac spoke volumes. It said everything I wanted to say to the world, "I am in charge!" I wanted to be the one driving up to a job site in that Cadillac as the owner and hear the contractor say, "Yes, sir" like that to me. I was certain that if I had that car, my dad would respect me like he respected Mr. Heymann.

That was the seed that was planted early on. We often forget our childhood dreams, but I held onto this one. Perhaps we shouldn't let those dreams fade away. Little did I know how it was going to define so much of my life.

No one said anything to make me think it was anything, but possible. I was raised in a home where Dad and Mom always said, "You can be anything you want to be." They would say, "We believe in you, and there is nothing you can't do." It was then in about 1966 that the impression was set, constant confidence, without ever knowing how or what I would do to be that person one day — the owner of a building and pulling up to a job site in a new Cadillac. At the time, the Cadillac signified success.

Automotive Status Symbol

The Cadillac's status symbol is among one of the first automobile brands in the world, second in the United States only to fellow General Motors marque Buick. By the time GM purchased the company in 1909, Cadillac already had established itself as one of America's premier luxury car makers and laid the foundation for the modern mass production of automobiles. It was at the forefront of technological advances, introducing full electrical systems, with its V8, setting the standard for the American automotive industry.

Cadillac produced the first American-made car to win the British Royal Automobile Club's Dewar Trophy, by successfully demonstrating the inter-exchangeability of its component parts during a reliability test in 1908; this spawned the firm's slogan: "Standard of the World." Cadillac won the trophy again in 1912 for incorporating electric starting and lighting in a production automobile.

To me, a Cadillac meant happiness. I thought that if I had X, Y, or Z, I would be happy. Those dreams are good to have. They shape and motivate us as we work our way through the rat race to get to where we need to be — one way or another, dreams create the path we need to follow, even if we learn we belong somewhere else. I ended up owning more than 30 Cadillacs and I bought my dad a Cadillac convertible Allanté.

Acadian Heritage and High School

Dad was Cajun, a French Acadian. Although we were told the name East was Irish, it comes from Louisiana. My grandfather was born in Lake Charles and my grandmother was born in Church Point. My grandmother was 100 percent Cajun French. While my dad was the larger-than-life figure, my mother was a beautiful petite Italian woman. She was born and raised in Baton Rouge, Louisiana. Her maiden name was Bonanno, 100 percent Italian. Her grandmother and grandfather were born in Italy. So, I grew up enjoying Cajun French and Italian food, both heritages. I *never* went hungry.

One important distinction to make is that the term *créole* at the time was consistently used to signify native, or locally born in contrast to foreign born. French immigration was at its peak during the 17th and 18th centuries which firmly established the Creole culture and language in Louisiana. In general, the core of the population was rather diverse, coming from all over the French colonial empire, specifically Canada, France, and the French West Indies.

We mostly grew up spending our childhood surrounded by my mom's Italian side of the family. Our routine consisted of going to Catholic Mass on Sundays, and then lunch at my grandparents — meatballs and cannoli — always home-cooked Italian food. These times were consistent and comforting. When we spent time with the Cajun French family on my dad's side, we would always end up at his mother's home or my aunt and uncle's home. There was always gumbo, a crawfish boil, or seafood of some kind. The smells were wonderful, the aroma of the spices was welcoming and comforting, and to this day still reminds me of home.

I spent my early years in Lafayette and later Baton Rouge. In the summer of 1970, between eighth grade and my freshman year of high school, we moved to Pensacola Beach, Florida. We lived a charmed life on the beach in a small tourist town of maybe 3,000 people in the off-season. During the tourist season the population would swell to 8,000 or more. It was like living in Mayberry R.F.D., where everybody knew everybody else.
High school was fabulous. I attended Pensacola Catholic High School and to this day remain close to most of my high school friends. Our parents would allow us to throw house parties and invite all our friends over for the night. They even let us drink beer. Dad would say that we're going to drink with or without his permission, so he'd rather we stayed at

home where it was safe than to be out all hours of the night drinking and getting into trouble. At least if you are home you can't get into *too* much trouble.

Clark in Pensacola Beach in 1975

Mom and Dad would book a hotel room across the bay and let us have the house. They would come back in the morning and there would be kids passed out on the floor, couch, pool table, or wherever they landed during the night.

I spent a lot of time with my brother on the beach driving around and drinking beer. The local sheriff was friendly to us natives. He once caught me driving on the beach while drinking beer. He made me pour out the beer and told me to go right home, which I failed to do. When I finally went home early the next morning, I found him in our driveway, drinking coffee and talking to my mom.

I stayed busy as the freshman class president, playing football, tennis, and on the surf team. Yep, we had a surf team. It was a remarkable time to grow up in Pensacola.

Dad was renovating apartment complexes at that time and had bought a 120-unit complex in 1975 to renovate and sell, called Zangwood Villa in Oakcliff, Texas. During the summer of 1975 my brother Blaine and I, along with a few high school friends, worked for my dad renovating the two-story complex. One of the first things Dad did while renovations where underway was he went to Radio Shack and bought a box of security cameras that he strung around the villa but didn't hook up to a monitoring service. "Best deterrent to theft," Dad would say. We would get a little giddy watching the residents waving at the camera, combing their hair thinking the cameras were hooked up. My high school friends who worked with us nicknamed my dad, "Big Daddy," because he was larger than life, and the absolute hands-on voice of authority.

How did we go from Florida to Louisiana then Dallas? We attended high school in Florida, worked for the summer at an apartment complex in Dallas for Dad, then attended college in Louisiana that fall.

> *We did not realize it at the time but were living during a unique time in history. It was between 1970 and 1975, and the Vietnam war was coming to an end. Nixon was president, and Motown was the best music to exist, along with all the artists of the 1970s. It was indeed quite a time to be alive, even if I didn't realize I was living during such a rich time in history.*

Chapter 2
PUMPED UP COLLEGE DAYS

After graduating from high school, my dad bought me my first car. We went down to the dealership, and I brought home a brand-new Corvette. It was a sexy little machine, and in my mind I could see girls lined up wanting to ride with me. Then mom protested our decision, so back to the dealership we went.

Clark's high school graduation photo in 1975

She said that there was too much plastic and fiberglass and not enough steal to protect my little head if I were to get into an accident. My second choice, a new-to-me Hurst Oldsmobile, was a classic choice and I enjoyed it almost as much. I studied pre-med at Louisiana State University (LSU) in Baton Rouge and was determined to be a pediatrician, but that meant getting up early every morning for biology class, which did not fit into my social schedule as well as I had first imagined.

My sister Sue, the all-natural, long blonde haired, 5′ 6″ fashion Barbie, sported a new Lincoln Continental Cartier. She was my serious, drop-dead gorgeous, model-material, football-player-dating, roommate from the second floor of a 900-square-foot, two-bedroom apartment on the edge of the Tigerland Apartment Complex. One of my best friends from high school, Mercedes Jackson, who was like a second sister to me, moved from Pensacola to Baton Rouge and moved in with us like the 1980's TV show *Three's Company*. It was free communal living, walking around in my underwear, with loving parents paying rent, utilities, food — keeping us comfortable. It was our small utopian island just off the coast of reality.

While my days were all about my classes, my nights were full of social engagements and obligations, visiting friends in bars and generally tooling around town with my older brother Blaine. He was my partner in crime *and* my best friend. I knew that if I were in trouble, he would be the guy to bail me out. We usually were together searching through the social scene at LSU after class. Blaine was about my height, but a little thinner with a long mustache like Tom Selleck. Like me, he was a sharp dresser, always fashionable with dress shoes, slacks, and a stylish, button-down shirt that boasted a little horse above the pocket. He always had a mind for big concepts. He lived at our grandparent's house, so he did not have to pay rent either.

We were very well protected from the realities of poverty. We didn't flaunt it, but it was evident that we had resources that were simply unavailable to most of our fellow classmates. Our family was just like the family on the show *Dallas*. Dad was Jock Ewing, who called all of us "Boo," from time to time. Cajun term of endearment for a family member is "Boo," it means love in Cajun French. Blaine was like J.R. Ewing, I was like Bobby, Sis was Sue, and mom was… *well*, Miss Ellie.

Things did not go as well as I had anticipated during the first part of my freshman year at LSU. So, one night, my brother and I were making our rounds through the bars, driving from one traffic light to the next, when Blaine came up with the rational idea to start our own bar and sandwich shop. It was the perfect marriage of our lifelong passions, partying with friends, eating, and drinking beer. Seemed like a win-win and before one could say, *Geaux Tigers*, Blaine found a closed-down gas station with an apartment on top. Blaine named it The Pump-N-Station because of the old gas pumps. He created the menu, filled with all the gas-station-themed cuisine that anyone could bear in a single sitting.

It was simple math to assume we would run it together with our sister Sue. All I wanted to do was cook. Blaine was the hands-on contractor and promoter, and our beautiful sister, who everyone wanted to date, ran the front end.

As fortune would have it, Dad was working as a general contractor remodeling a motel and apartment complex in

Shreveport, Louisiana, at that time. He invited Blaine and I to go to Shreveport and load up all the material we would need to remodel the place. Dad and Mom gave us the money for the start-up costs (around $7,000), and the rest was all free material and labor. Blaine and I did all the remodeling.

Blaine, Sue, and I were all given new cars for graduation. However, I was the only one of the three who ended up putting my 1975 Hurst Olds title at the local bank as collateral on a $10,000 loan. At the time, Blaine had a 1973 Regal Buick, and Sue had a 1974 Cutlass Supreme. When I look back on our first foray into business ownership, I often wonder why it was *my* car that was put up for collateral?

The Pump-N-Station was a big success. We served draft beer and New Orleans' style po'boys. Our number-one seller was the roast beef French dip, which my maternal grandfather, Vince Bonanno, taught me how to cook. I was the head cook at the Pump-N-Station. We served 100 to 150 po'boy sandwiches *just* at lunchtime each day. We opened at 10 a.m. and closed at 2 a.m. We sold 30 to 40 kegs of beer on Friday and Saturday nights. We had a courtyard that held about 250 people, and it stayed packed on Friday and Saturday, football nights, and game days. We offered live music and bands that played in the courtyard.

Blaine hired this big, overweight, jolly, misplaced hippie named Steve to help us out. Everyone loved Steve and Steve loved everyone. He was 6'2" with long brown hair, and a local backwoods bohemian, who always wore an untucked T-shirt, jean shorts, tennis shoes, and a smile on his face. Steve was a hard worker who knew the job backwards and forwards. He took a workload off our shoulders and managed the day-to-day operations like a professional.

Everyone wanted to be in our little pub on Friday nights. Sue was dating a star football player for the Tigers and after the game, he and his entourage would come in. His friends brought in their fans as well and the numbers would double every hour until about 3 a.m. when we usually ran out of beer, as well as leaded or unleaded po'boy sandwiches.

Blaine came up with brilliant marketing ideas for the Pump-n-Station. The first idea was to give every sorority free drink tickets. Naturally, all the fraternity boys would follow just so they could be with the girls. It worked flawlessly. We had 100 sorority girls and 200 fraternity guys every Friday night. It was the hottest place to be on the south side of LSU's campus. We only sat 30 people inside yet could fit 300 outside. People would flood the street and overflow crowds were inside the patio courtyard.

The second greatest marketing idea was Dad-inspired. We decided to have an honor system in place that stated once someone bought 100 beers, we had a brass name plaque made and mounted on the bar. We paid for the brass-engraved nameplate, but the advertising was better than Facebook is today. Everyone all over LSU wanted their name engraved on the brass name plaque mounted on the bar. Dad took this idea from a bar that he remodeled at The Court of Two Sisters in New Orleans. In fact, his name plaque is *still* there.

Another idea that came from Dad was to mount a Kotex machine in the women's bathroom and give the product away for free. This was before tampons came out, and long before the petitions fighting for free women's health products. It worked. Dad said women would remember a bar and restaurant certainly for its food and service, but more for the cleanliness of a restroom. Throw in free Kotex, and they will tell all their friends about it. It created a sense of respect for the business. In fact, women were by far our most successful word-of-mouth team for The Pump-N-Station — more so than the men.

One afternoon, as I was cleaning and setting up for the evening, I *accidently* fell in love with the new bartender, a *stunning* lady named Elaine. She was a junior at LSU and was hired part-time by Steve a few weeks prior — *remember I was just a freshman*. Elaine was a beautiful, athletic, LSU tennis player. She had beautiful long brown hair, wore tennis shoes and shorts, and kept her nails trimmed short. She was the first female trainer at LSU, providing physical therapy for the football team.

One Friday night, the Pump-N-Station was abuzz with energy from the college crowd. Elaine was pumping a draft beer from the tap and it was foaming over. I approached her and gently tipped the glass with my hand and told her to tilt the glass when filling it up, so it won't foam as much.

She looked over at what was clearly a very unimpressive cook, and said, "Hi, my name is Elaine." I replied, "Hi, my name is Clark."

She asked, "What do you do here?"

"Well, I own the place with my brother and sister," I replied. Which subsequently led to a lot of dating and a lot of great conversations. However, our first date didn't go as planned. I was supposed to be at her place for a barbecue, but I couldn't get away from the bar till after 10 p.m. That should tell you something about me, and it should have told me something about myself, too.

After running The Pump-N-Station for several months, I dropped out of LSU. I thought I didn't need college since I was making money and learning firsthand real business skills and entrepreneurship — more than any book could ever teach me. In fact, many famous businessmen and CEOs were college dropouts. We made $80,000 in our first year in business. It became immediately apparent that I was not going to become the family doctor and switch my major to construction technology before finally dropping out along with my brother. I knew the direction I wanted to go, even if I didn't know how I was going to get there, I knew I would. Blaine already had dropped out, although he went back later and finished his degree. Sister Sue also had dropped out and married a geologist. Blaine met his wife, Cathy, at The Pump-N-Station, and after a year and a half, he and Cathy got married and moved to Dallas. My parents had recently moved to Dallas from Pensacola Beach, so my dad could work on several apartment projects that he remodeled and owned. Blaine left me with The Pump-N-Station full-time. At that point, Sue was only working part-time and going to school full-time. I was left to run The Pump-N-Station all on my own at the young age of 19.

Another six months passed, and we already had a second small kiosk (drive-up only) Pump-N-Station, located in an apartment and bar community called Tigerland. We sold that unit and only had the original location to manage.

Driving a Second Business

About eight months into The Pump-N-Station business, I met a limo owner who had the only limo business in Baton Rouge. He would chauffeur all these famous bands that came to LSU and Baton Rouge. As it turned out, Elaine's professor was Dr. Broussard, who was also in charge of the LSU Assembly Center, where all the concerts were held. Elaine said she would talk to Dr. Broussard about her boyfriend, Clark East, to see if it was possible to provide a limo for all concerts.

Much to my gratitude, the doc said, "For you, Elaine, anything."

I then had an exciting opportunity to be the limo company for all the concerts at LSU. I called Dad and Mom, and said, "I'd like to buy a limo and open a limo company." As with any other dream of mine, my parents were nothing but supportive. My dad found a black 1973 Cadillac Limo in like-new condition. This was 1976, so the car wasn't that old at the time. It cost $3,500 — cash. My parents put up the money for me, and all of a sudden I had a second business. At just 19 years old, I had achieved success that most only dream of in their entire lifetime. That was just the beginning of my success.

I chauffeured all the bands and entertainers that performed at LSU. This included the Commodores (Lionel Richie), Neil Diamond, Willie Nelson, Rita Coolidge, Chris Christopherson,

Waylon Jennings, Gino Vanelli, Chicago, John Denver, War, Wild Cherry, Brothers Johnson, Herbie Hancock, and Three Dog Night. You can imagine how exciting this was for a young man of my age. The experience was something I will never forget. Imagine meeting your favorite celebrity at such a young age — and not only meeting them *yet* chauffeuring them around? It was surreal!

Limousine Clark bought to chauffeur the bands at LSU

Once, there was a Battle of the Bands at the New Orleans Superdome and Southern University, and I got to chauffeur the bands between New Orleans and Baton Rouge. During the Battle of the Bands, I was standing backstage next to Lionel Richie and Herbie Hancock. I was the only white guy in the entire auditorium when Herbie Hancock turned to Lionel Richie and said, "Isn't this *something*? We have a *white* chauffeur."

At the time, Blaine and my dad were saying, "You have to come to Dallas. It's vibrant, exciting, and you can make it big in Dallas." Since moving to Dallas, Dad was making a killing. Elaine had just graduated from LSU with a major in physical education, with a minor in math, hated her job, and succumbed to my parents' campaign for us to visit.

Chapter 3
MARRIAGE AND CAREER CHANGE

Elaine and I had talked about moving to Dallas to better our fortunes. Elaine read an ad in the *Dallas Morning News* that the Garland Independent School District was hiring teachers. She saw this as an exciting opportunity, so she responded to the ad and was immediately offered a job. This time I must have said something to impress her since she agreed to marry me. She proclaimed, "Okay, let's get married and move to Dallas!"

We went back to Baton Rouge, and I tried to sell The Pump-N-Station. A month passed and I still could not find a buyer, so we closed it down. I regret not trying to keep it open. It was a great run, though, and I learned a lot in a small amount of time.

Until I wrote this book, I didn't understand why I was the only investor sibling who used my own car for collateral on the loan for the Pump-N-Station. Maybe by the end of this book, I will reveal the answer. I was the only one always giving first.

I have always considered myself to be self-sacrificing and determined; what a dangerous combination that can be. I'm glad I did though because every little step, every little choice, can be a stepping-stone to one's ideal destination. I deeply regretted closing the bar, but I made 100 times more in commercial real estate than what I made in the bar-restaurant endeavor.

Clark and Elaine at their wedding in 1978

I already had proposed to Elaine, and now we needed to speed up the process. I went to her dad and asked permission to marry his daughter. All he said was, "Son, do you love her?" I said, "yes, sir!" And he said, "That's all I needed to hear."

Two years after our first conversation we were married in Baton Rouge, and within a two-week span, immediately following our honeymoon in The Bahamas, we moved to Dallas. Elaine took a job teaching math at Garland High School, and I got a job as a punch-out foreman with my dad's construction company.

MARRIAGE AND CAREER CHANGE

East Family in 1984 — Elaine and Clark eventually had three beautiful babies

Brendan East   *Jamie East Billig*   *Jonathan East*

When a construction project is nearly completed, the customer or his representative inspects the work and writes a list of concerns, such as flaws, errors, or requirements, that have not yet been addressed. This list is called a "punch list." The person assigned to fix the problems identified on the list is a punchout foreman and is required to have a lot of experience with different responsibilities and jobs on a construction site. I was the punchout foreman.

Clark and Elaine in front of their home in Plano, Texas in 1984

My responsibilities were basically completing the finish work — mainly taking care of electrical and plumbing problems. This could involve correcting problems with electrical outlets, as well as adjusting or replacing electrical fixtures. Sometimes the building was almost ready for the owner to take possession by the time I got the punch list tasks or was moving in and stepping over me to place furniture and install appliances. All that time spent with my dad on his job sites taught me just about every job on a construction site. I was practically a journeyman with good basic skills for every trade on a construction site. Painting was the last step after drywall and carpentry work was completed. Punchout technicians often need to paint a wall, perform minor touchup painting, or paint wood trim. Painting is typically one of the final tasks for the technician.

After the carpenters, painters, and electricians left a newly constructed house or other building for the last time, I took over. I was also responsible for repairs as part of final quality control. Quality control required an eye for detail and a meticulous approach to work. I handled the final punch list as each apartment was finished and turned over to management to begin renting the units out to a new tenant. I was usually the last one out the door and off the job site every night. On my way home, I would fill up my car, grab a soda, or beer, and head home.

Texas-Sized Business Influence

During one trip through the checkout lane at the grocery, I spotted a copy of *Texas Monthly* magazine and on its cover was a big picture of a Texas-sized successful businessman named Sherwood Blount. He was a real estate broker who recently inked a multi-million-dollar deal. The story addressed how he started from scratch and built a sizable development company. I immediately felt a connection to this guy. I'm not much of a reader, but I've always been keenly interested in stories about successful people. I was the one in the family, even though I knew construction, who did not get my hands dirty. I would be the company owner.

The story began, when Sherwood was a kid, one Saturday morning in the winter of 1961, he went into the kitchen of his parents' small, neat, white, clapboard house in East Dallas and asked his mother for a quarter so he could go to the afternoon double feature at the Arcadia Theatre. "Honey," she told him, "I don't have a quarter. Daddy doesn't get paid till Monday. It's not in the budget." That was when Sherwood decided he wanted not *just* as much money as his daddy had — enough to eat and live in a house — but enough so he could always go to the movies, enough to buy a Chevrolet, enough to eat at Kip's Big Boy every night, enough to join the Lakewood Country Club and play golf. Even as a boy he knew that the main worry in the lives of his parents and his grandparents was not having enough money. He knew the whole point of the hard work they did all day was money, and that even so there was never enough.
(source: Texasmonthly.com/articles/sherwood-blounts-first-million)

> *"In the long run men only hit what they aim at. Therefore, though they should fail immediately, they had better aim at something high."*
> *—Henry David Thoreau*

The article went on to talk about a few of the multimillion-dollar deals that Sherwood orchestrated throughout the Dallas area, his successes, and ability to recognize lucrative real estate opportunities. Sherwood Blount was as poor as a church mouse. He did, however, have a powerful determination and drive. This man believed in himself and was a self-made millionaire at the age of 28. He was the president of his own real estate brokerage firm, the owner of two 1979 Cadillacs, and a brand-new house in the Dallas suburbs. I wrote him a letter. He wrote me back and said don't ever give up on your dream and invited me to see him anytime.

That was me all over. I had the willingness, drive, and vision to make this happen for myself. Nothing could stop me from my destination. I thought of the vision and feeling I had when I was 10 years old. I knew that I wanted to be the owner of shopping centers or office buildings, because I knew I would be the one driving to the site in my new Fleetwood Cadillac. Seeing Sherwood Blount in the magazine's article with a new Cadillac, I decided it was time for me to pursue my dream.

I went to work the next day and told my dad I wanted to quit the construction job with him. With confidence, I explained that I wanted to start my own company and become a shopping center developer. Being the supportive father that he was, my dad replied, "Okay, this is what you need to do..."

> *"She did not stand alone, but what stood behind her, the most potent moral force in her life, was the love of her father."*
> —Harper Lee

My dad went on to tell me exactly what I needed to do to start this new journey in my life. He informed me that I would need to form a Sub-S Corporation and find a small piece of property on which to start my first project. He went on to say that I will need to put together a Pro-forma. Now, I had no idea what a shopping center Pro-forma looked like or even consisted of. It was a lot of information to process, and I'm glad that I had the guidance of my father. It wasn't an easy task to own shopping centers nor office buildings, and even with my father's guidance, I knew I would need more help if I was going to successfully manage this.

"You first have to start with the size of the land. The land size determines the size of the center," my father said. I listened intently to every bit of advice and wisdom he had to offer, as I formulated the next steps of my plan.

My next step was to call Sherwood Blount's office and ask for an appointment. To my surprise, he agreed to see me and invited me to meet with him.

I had to start somewhere, and Sherwood could give me the additional guidance I sought. I arrived at his office, eager to learn. Sherwood welcomed me and dived right into the basics. He said I should start with a small piece of property in a secondary market to gain learning experience. Sherwood would say that the keys to these deals, besides persistence and hard work, were relationships and commitment.

He then introduced me to a real estate broker from his office named Rusty McDearman. Rusty was a successful broker at the ripe age of 30. He was a tall, red-headed, defensive player for SMU, easy to get along with, and had the knowledge and experience I needed to make my first purchase. Because of this networking opportunity, I was able to find a one-acre commercial-zoned property in Grapevine, Texas, with an asking price of $120,000 for the site. I signed a contract to buy the site in my new company's name, CDE Investments INC. (CDE stood for Clark D. East) I did not have two nickels to rub together, but I had a dream and determination — and with that, anything was possible!

At that time, as a high school teacher, Elaine earned about $25,000 a year. I earned about the same. We had a new baby girl, and we lived in a two-bedroom apartment. We had one new car (Regal Buick) payment, rent, and utilities. We also recently had bought a TV, baby furniture, a new mattress and box spring, as well as a new sofa. It seemed that we were rich, but we had only a few dollars remaining after each paycheck. Despite our lack of funds, Elaine was 100 percent supportive of me quitting my job to start my own company. I had no experience, nor did I know how I could borrow enough to build a shopping center from scratch. It was through blind faith and God that I took those first steps. I never had one doubt nor worry that I would not nor could not make it happen. We hear a lot about the Law of Attraction and the power of positive thinking, and this is my real-life experience. All I did was wake up and say to myself that I would find a way to get it done. This is how blind faith — and in my opinion — God works. When you believe that what you are doing is right, some way, somehow, without even knowing how, things start to fall into place.

After putting the one-acre site under contract, I finished the Pro-forma and learned that with one acre (43,560 square feet of land), I could build 10,000 square feet of shopping center space. That included all the required setbacks, retention, landscaping, pond or drainage area, and parking lot with the required number of parking spaces to accommodate a 10,000-square-foot center. These first few steps required a lot of planning and attention to detail, and I quickly learned a great deal about real estate and the business of owning shopping centers.

Once everything was in place, I was ready to start calling on prospective tenants. Sherwood Blount and Rusty McDearman helped me tremendously by introducing me to my first anchor tenant. I realized how helpful having these connections were to my business. Reaching out and networking with the right people cannot be underestimated in any business field. As I researched tenants, I had a particular area of focus.

Shopping Centers of Milk and Honey

The anchor tenant is the drawing card for the entire center. In this case it was a Schepps Dairy convenience store. For those who have never had the pleasure to know Schepps, it was similar to a local market store. The grocery was a little bigger than a convenience store, such as 7-Eleven, yet smaller than the mega markets where we can get lost searching for a decent brand of creamer for our morning coffee.

Founded by Harmon Schepps in 1942, Schepps Dairy employed about 550 local employees, many of whom worked in a state-of-the-art manufacturing facility in the shadow of downtown. The growing grocery business had long been promoted as "the dairy best," which was a pretty catchy slogan. I called Schepps Dairy and met with Pete Schenkel, the president and owner, and proposed my location for their next grocery store. He agreed.

The site plan and elevation depicted a 10,000-square-foot center with a convenience store at the corner, including four gas pumps and a canopy. Schepps Dairy would be the anchor tenant. Next, I secured a dry cleaner, hair salon, coin-operated laundromat, insurance agency, and video rental tenant. This was in 1980 and way before Blockbuster video even existed. Mr. Schenkel said he would take the end cap space (2,500 square feet) at eight dollars per square foot. At that time, interest rates were (prime borrowing rate) 18 to 19 percent, so eight dollars per square foot was a great rental rate. I was asking $10 per square foot for an anchor tenant, since it's the best location and greatest visibility in the entire center.

Mr. Schenkel asked me if I wanted a gross lease or a net lease. I said gross, because I assumed just like gross income, a gross lease meant more.

Mr. Schenkel started laughing and said, "Are you sure?" I said, "Yes, sir."

Thankfully, Mr. Schenkel gave me a bit of a real-estate lesson. He went on to explain the difference of a gross lease and a net or triple net lease, saying, "young man, you want only triple net leases."

You see a gross lease means the landlord pays for everything. The landlord pays all or most expenses associated with the property, including taxes, insurance, and maintenance out of the rents received from tenants. Utilities and landscape services are included within one easy, tenant-friendly rent payment. So, if the tenant is a big consumer of electricity, it could be very costly for a landlord. In a net lease, or triple net lease, the landlord charges a base rent for the commercial space, plus some or all usual costs — expenses associated with operations and maintenance. These can include real-estate taxes, property insurance, as well as common area maintenance items (CAMS), such as janitorial services, property management fees, sewer, water, trash collection, landscaping, parking lots, fire sprinklers, and any commonly shared area or service. In this case, the tenant pays the eight dollars per square foot annually for his 2,500-square-foot space. This means the tenant also pays for his own electricity, utilities, CAM fee, and pro-rata share of the real estate taxes.

It was clear that what I really wanted was a triple net lease. We laughed about this for quite some time. No one bothered to tell me about gross or net leases prior to this, and I did not know enough to ask. I will always be grateful for this man's honesty that prevented me from making a huge financial mistake that I surely would have regretted later. I had a lot of great people supporting and helping me through the process. This support, along with my own determination, continued to propel me throughout this experience.

Mr. Pete Schenkel was one of the most honest, caring, and giving people I've ever met. I remember in 1973, a Schepps' worker was killed during a robbery at a company-owned convenience store. Mr. Schenkel put up a reward, which helped crack the case, and the company continued doing it.

Jamaison Schuler, company spokesperson, said, "It may get some violent criminal off the street a little bit quicker." That alone is a pretty good reason to leverage a few bucks for the safety of the neighborhoods and communities in the urban areas. But it's not like Mr. Schenkel was doing it for PR purposes, offering up as much as $10,000 rewards in many recent high-profile crimes. Any major PR campaign could risk employee safety and could adversely affect a witnesses' credibility in a trial. Over a 40-year timeframe, the company paid nearly $1.5 million in reward money, and because of those rewards, there was an indictment in more than 100 local cases.

At the time, all I needed to get was a $300,000 loan. I had my whole package together. I opened up the phone book and started looking up banks in Dallas — there was no internet nor Google in 1980! I went to 32 banks in an effort to secure a loan. They all said no. Others may have taken this as a sign and succumbed to defeat, but my parents taught me to never give up — no matter what. I continued my search, and finally found a bank named the National Bank of Commerce in downtown Dallas.

My routine had been to arrive at the bank without an appointment, sit in the lobby, and ask to see the president of the bank. My dad always said to start at the top.

Back then, the secretary would ask if I had an appointment, and I'd say, "No, ma'am." She would say the president had an appointment and wouldn't be available for another hour. I'd say, "That's okay, I'll sit and wait."

And I did. I waited patiently at all 32 banks. One banker after another would see me and say I have no experience, no assets nor collateral, and *if* I get a center built, along with a track record, come back and see them. It was the all too common, "you must have the experience to get experience." All logic was against me. Who would give me a loan without collateral? Without experience?

Finally, the 33rd bank, National Bank of Commerce, said *yes*. That was if I had someone to co-sign the loan. I then had to find someone willing to co-sign a $300,000 loan. I did not allow this to be another rejection. I knew I would find a way to make this opportunity work. Through blind faith and God, I continued. Against all odds, I had no doubt that I would find a way to make it work.

Chance Encounter

Often people in our lives have been placed carefully, whether it is for their benefit or our own. Think of the people who have supported you or given you a chance when no one else would. Yet again, I watched as all the uncertain pieces of my journey fell into place. At the time, Elaine was teaching high school geometry at Garland High. One day after school, as she walked around Valley View Mall in North Dallas, she saw a nicely dressed woman with a Mary Kay pin on her blazer. Elaine approached this woman to ask her about Mary Kay cosmetics. It was a simple act that opened many doors. The lady turned out to be married to a real estate developer and investor. Her name was Gloria Blanchard. Gloria invited Elaine to her home for a Mary Kay facial and demonstration. At that same time, Elaine let Gloria know that I was looking for an investor or partner. Gloria said she would tell her husband about me and that I was looking for an investor to build a shopping center. It is often small choices that lead to greatness.

Elaine returned home excited to tell me about Mary Kay and how she became a Mary Kay rep. Not only that, but the woman she met in the mall was married to a real estate developer/investor who would be willing to meet me. When

I met Ray Blanchard and showed him my proposed shopping center, I told the story of how I went to 32 banks. All of which turned me down, but the 33rd bank, National Bank of Commerce, said yes — subject to a guarantor co-signing the loan with me.

From left, Glenn Lyons, Clark East, and FairTex Builders' Contractor in 1983 at the High Point Village groundbreaking, the center that Clark sold to Ross Perot

Ray said, "Well, son, what a small world! I know Harry McCaffrey at National Bank of Commerce, and he knows me well." He then asked, "Who are you dealing with at the bank?"

I confidently answered, "Harry McCaffrey." I had already made my way to the top, but Ray didn't stop at that. He said, "Tell Harry I'll do the deal with you." And all of this happened simply because I didn't give up, though it seemed I had every reason to. We hear a lot of stories about holding onto a dream despite rejection. We see these show up on our social media feeds, featured in the news, and hear them as subjects at our favorite TED Talks, yet it doesn't always fall into place.

We built a 10,000-square-foot shopping center called Mustang Plaza located on Mustang Drive in Grapevine. We built it for $300,000 and sold it for $700,000 just six months after completion to a Taiwanese buyer who was an engineer at Texas Instruments.

Ray Blanchard continued to work with me for several years. We went on to build two more shopping centers and an office building. I was a millionaire at the mere age of 25. My brother Blaine joined us and then my dad. We then started a development company together, whereby I handled all the financing and banking (loans). Blaine handled the design, leasing, and permitting. My dad handled the construction.

This was my first shopping center. It was the first step that led to a lucrative career and a series of events I could never have imagined. We went on to develop four more shopping centers. In 1982 my dad and brother found a 120-room historic hotel to buy in downtown Dallas, called the Ambassador Park Hotel. We bought it for $2.75 million but needed a $10 million loan to renovate the hotel. We had a $150,000 earnest money deposit, which was live and forfeitable on the hotel contract, and we needed a $12.5 million loan to close in 30 days. A real estate broker introduced me to a savings and loan called Sunbelt Savings and Loan. They issued a take-out commitment, which meant I still needed a bank or lender to loan me the interim (construction and acquisition loan), and once the construction remodeling was finished, Sunbelt would provide permanent financing.

Four days before our contract was expiring when we would have lost the $150,000 earnest money deposit, I found Killeen Savings and Loan out of Killeen, Texas. They agreed to approve me for a $12.5 million loan and could close in three days. Securing a 12-million-dollar loan in four days was difficult, but not out of the norm during this time since banks, and especially savings and loans, were trying to loan as much money as they could. The reason for this was that they could charge upfront points and participate in a project.

Texas Legend Steps In

During that year, I also developed a shopping center in Dallas on Greenville Avenue called High Point Village. I was outside the center sweeping the parking lot when a Mercedes pulled up, the driver's side window slowly rolled down and a gentleman poked his head out and asked, "Do you know who the owner is?"

I said, "I am." *Keep in mind, I was only 25 at the time.* He introduced himself as Merv Stauffer, and that he represented H. Ross Perot, and he wanted to buy my center.

Mr. Perot's own business successes were awe-inspiring. Born and raised in Texarkana, Texas, he was a true Texas legend. Mr. Perot left the Navy in 1957 and became a salesman for IBM. He quickly became a top employee — one year, he fulfilled his annual sales quota in a mere two weeks — and tried to pitch his ideas to supervisors who largely ignored him. He left IBM in 1962 and founded Electronic Data Systems (EDS) in Dallas and courted large corporations for his data processing services. I learned that Mr. Perot was denied bids for contracts 77 times before receiving his first contract — that's persistence and determination. EDS received lucrative contracts from the U.S. government in the 1960s, computerizing Medicare records. EDS went public in 1968, and the stock price rose from $16 a share to $160 within days. *Fortune* called Ross Perot the "fastest, richest Texan" in a 1968 cover story. In 1984, General Motors bought a controlling interest in EDS for $2.4 billion.

Mr. Perot was expanding into other interest and ventures. He established Perot Systems in 1988 and was an angel investor for NeXT, a computer company founded by Steve Jobs after he left Apple. Mr. Perot also became heavily involved in the Vietnam War POW/MIA issue, arguing that hundreds of American servicemen were left behind in Southeast Asia after the Vietnam War. During the presidency of George H. W. Bush, Mr. Perot became increasingly active in politics and strongly opposed the Gulf War and ratification of the North American Free Trade Agreement. In 1992, Mr. Ross Perot announced his intention to run for president of the United States and advocated a balanced budget, an end to the outsourcing of jobs, and the enactment of electronic direct democracy.

Mr. Stauffer said that a broker, Bob Hydeman, would represent the sale and would contact me in a few days. Mr. Hydeman called the next day asked how much I wanted for the center. I told him $5 million, at a 6.5 cap rate, unheard of at the time. We built the center for $4.2 million and sold it for $5 million. My partner was Glen Lyons, and we had a 50/50 split. Mr. Stauffer said, "We'll send the papers over today." A Hotshot driver pulled up with a contract that included earnest money in the form of a personal check, signed by H. Ross Perot for $50,000, to close in 30 days.

Mr. Perot and I met in his conference room. The documents were sitting on the table waiting for his signature. We shook hands and he sat down to read the stack of papers, ran down the list of fully leased property, and signed the contract to buy my shopping center, High Point Village, a mere 30 days after meeting his broker, Bob Hydeman. The Ross Perot family still owns the center today. Mr. Ross Perot told me, "I always hired people smarter than me, I would hire an Eagle Scout before I would hire a college graduate, he has all the qualities I want in an employee."

Mr. Hydeman became my mentor, and he and I remained best friends for 40 years. After I met and sold High Point Village to Mr. Perot, I joint ventured with the Perot Pension Fund for two years on three more projects.

Because of that meeting, I was given an opportunity for the Perot Company Pension Fund to become my funding partner, so no more bank financing. I would have been better off with Mr. Perot, owning 50 percent of 100 deals rather than owning 100 percent of 10 deals. Vanity set in, however, and I convinced myself that I could do all this myself and didn't need to share 50 percent of the deals with anyone. Boy was I wrong.

I remember a cold call from a young 26-year-old real estate broker named Sonny Molloy out of Atlanta. I gave him his first listing in Florida on a Tires Plus I had developed in Estero, Florida. Sonny not only sold the Tires Plus for me but went on to sell virtually every project I developed over the next 10 years (approximately $30 million in projects). It all started with a cold call. One of my first cold calls was to the Outback Steakhouse real estate department. I called for weeks until I finally got a real estate manager named Carl Sahlsten, who gave me my first Outback site to do a build-to-suit Outback Steakhouse in Port St. Lucie, Florida. Persistence, persistence, persistence. Never, never, never give up.

Right Place. Right Time. Right People.

This is all another example of how everything seemed to fall into place, even when I wasn't necessarily looking. The friendships and business connections I made during my real estate experience were priceless. I believe God led these people into my life for a reason, and it is through blind faith and seemingly foolish hope that I achieved what I did. If you think you can't achieve your dreams, think again. Look at the people you already know and never give up hope.

Whether it's someone with whom you can network to further your career or business, or simply someone who inspires and supports you no matter what, they are in your life for a reason. Find them, recognize them, and nourish those friendships and connections. You may not know how you're going to get where you want to go, but the path exists — you just need to find it!

IMPOSSIBLE CAN'T STOP ME !

My favorite toy was a 42-foot Regal 4080 Sportyacht. Bought new, this motorized condo would set you back $480,000, today would be worth $800,000. In 2006, I bought the boat from the previous owner for $125,000, by taking over his payments. I renamed the boat, Against All Odds.

Imperfect Action

I did not know then that I was setting the stage. I could always pull things out of my ass at the 11th hour, so in 2010 when I took money from the trust account of which I was trustee that led to my conviction and later imprisonment, I thought I could pull it out of my ass again at the 11th hour. I had so much to learn. The bottom line is, dishonest *is* dishonest, and wrong *is* wrong. There is no justification for what I did and put my family through, which will be revealed as you continue to read.

> *"Start by doing what's necessary; then do what's possible; and suddenly you are doing the impossible."*
> — *Francis of Assisi*

Believe in Yourself and Your Dreams

Back to my dream of being the proud owner of a Cadillac, I'd like to present you with a challenge of sorts. I ask that you ponder your early life decisions and the hopes and dreams you once had, or perhaps still have. What dreams helped shape your life?

You may think it's not possible and that they are simply wishes of a childish heart, one foolish enough to believe that anything can happen. But you know what? What seems to be a miracle can and will happen. What's the catch? You simply *must* believe in yourself. You *must* believe that you can achieve *anything*. The power of belief isn't just an idea; it's scientific. Statistically speaking, you are likely to have more success when you believe you will succeed. Think of salesmen who assume the close — it might even seem hopeless that this random person they are cold-calling will buy their product, buy with confidence, self-assurance, and that confidence in themselves leads even the most skeptical person to become a customer — a true fact and experience in my life.

Whatever IT is that you want to achieve, write IT down. It can be as simple as wanting a new car and knowing you can't afford it yet or something as big as your dream home or dream job. After you've jotted this down, don't worry about planning how you will achieve it. That can come later. Just know that you will.

Chapter 4
RISE AND FALL OF THE SAVINGS AND LOAN (S&L)

From 1982 through 1985, the economy was thriving. Although signs of a recession were looming, it was a great time to be in commercial real estate until the bottom began to drop out. Interest rates were dropping, but the real estate market was tremendously overbuilt. When President Ronald Reagan deregulated savings and loans to help spur the economy, real estate went through the ceiling due to easy borrowing and no real guidelines to which a loan was approved or underwritten. This meant that most banks required at least 40 to 50 percent preleasing before they would fund a loan.

S&L lending was never lax in bringing a deal, any deal, that even came close to making sense, pre-leasing or not. S&Ls would charge four to six points, which is four to six percent of the total amount of the loan at closing. This would be paid out of the borrowers' loan amount (proceeds), so the S&L could make a profit the day they closed a loan. An average loan of $5 million would pay six points. That was $135,000 in addition to what the S&L would get from a loan participation fee or interest on the real estate project. An average was 25 percent participation.

Everyone was betting on the come. The S&L earned interest on the loan, six points to close the deal, and when the project was finished and sold, it would get 25 percent of the net profits. A developer did not care, myself included, since

I had financing and did not need to put any money down, so I did not need an equity partner. If I succeeded, I was happy to give the S&L part of my profits.

Unfortunately, every S&L in the country was loaning on speculative projects. The saying was, "see-through buildings and shopping centers." This meant that a developer could go through all the motions of building a new shopping center, which lacked tenants; shopping centers without opened stores; and other urban development projects with no real use or purpose. The insured financiers would get bailed out by the government.

> *"Bottoms in the investment world don't end with four-year lows; they end with 10 or 15-year lows."*
> *— Jim Rogers*

S&L Glory Fades

The S&L crisis was created when regulations were relaxed to help the country recover from a recession and avoid a depression. However, it did not take into account market conditions, speculation, as well as outright corruption and fraud. It also didn't consider the implementation of greatly slackened and broadened lending standards that led desperate banks to take far too much risk, balanced by far too little on-hand capital.
(source: By Will Kenton, https://www. investopedia.com)

In 1982, in response to the poor prospects for S&Ls under current economic conditions, President Ronald Reagan signed the Garn-St. Germain Depository Institutions Act, which eliminated loan-to-value ratios and interest rate caps for S&Ls. This allowed them to hold 30 percent of their assets in consumer loans and 40 percent in commercial loans. No longer were S&Ls hemmed in by regulations. Unlimited reward uncoupled from high risk.

S&Ls began investing in riskier commercial real estate and even riskier junk bonds. This strategy of investing in riskier projects and instruments assumed that they would pay off in higher returns. Of course, if those returns didn't materialize, it would be taxpayers through the Federal Savings and Loan Insurance Corporation (FSLIC) — not the banks nor S&L officials — who would be left holding the bag. That's exactly what eventually happened.

By 1985, some S&L assets had shot up by more than 50 percent — far faster growth than banks. S&L growth was especially robust in Texas. Some state legislators allowed S&Ls to double down by allowing them to invest in speculative real estate. By 1983, more than a third of S&Ls were not profitable. By 1987, the FSLIC had become insolvent. Rather than allow it and S&Ls to fail, as they were destined to do, the federal government recapitalized the FSLIC.

The relaxed regulations and sheer lack of responsibility and oversight opened a pandora's box of lies, fraud, and theft among S&L insiders. One common fraud saw two partners conspire with an appraiser to buy land using S&L loans and flip it to extract huge profits. Partner One would buy a parcel at its appraised market value. The duo would then conspire with an appraiser to have it reappraised at a far higher price.

The parcel would then be sold to Partner Two using a loan from an S&L, which was then defaulted on. Both partners and the appraiser would share the profits. Some S&Ls knew of — and allowed — such fraudulent transactions to happen.

Compounding this issue was the lack of understanding by the regulators to appreciate the nature and depth of the fraud. These complex cases went unabated for years, if not for the want, but for earnest understanding of the crime itself.

The S&L crisis is arguably the most catastrophic collapse of the banking industry since the Great Depression. Across the United States, more than 1,000 S&Ls had failed by 1989, essentially ending what had been one of the most secure sources of home mortgages. The S&L market share for single-family mortgages before the crisis was 53 percent in 1975, but by 1990, it had dropped to 30 percent.

The crisis was felt doubly hard in Texas where at least half of the failed S&Ls were based. The collapse of the S&L industry pushed the state into a severe recession. Faulty land investments were auctioned off, causing real estate prices to plummet. Office vacancies rose significantly, and the price of crude oil dropped by half. Texas banks, such as Empire Savings and Loan, took part in criminal activities that further caused the Texas economy to plummet. The bill for Empire's eventual default cost taxpayers about $300 million.

Finally, the recession took hold on the economy, and to make matters worse, The Tax Act of 1986, broadened the income tax base by wholesale elimination of tax preferences for individuals and corporations. The investment tax credit was repealed for property placed in service after December 31, 1985.
(source: *Investment. Volume 3, Lifting the Burden: Tax Reform, the Cost of Capital, and U.S. Economic Growth*, By Dale W. Jorgenson and Kun-Young Yun)

An example was a major airline corporation that was based in Dallas. One developer had more than 100 airlines and pilots in his real estate projects as limited partners, with each putting up to $10,000 for one percent interest in the real estate project. They did not care if the project *ever* made money, because the law before President Reagan changed it, allowing the investor to write off 10 times his investment. So, if the investor put in $10,000, he could write off $100,000. That meant his $100,000 salary was virtually tax-free.

By 1987 the FSLIC had become insolvent, and Monday, October 19, 1987 became known as *Black Monday*. On that day, stockbrokers in New York, London, Hong Kong, Berlin, Tokyo, and just about any other city with an exchange, stared at the figures running across the display with a growing sense of dread. A financial strut had buckled, and the strain brought world markets tumbling down.

By 1989, the new draconian tax laws, along with the overlending and overbuilding, brought the U.S. into a deep recession. S&Ls were going out of business and taken over by the FDIC daily. President George H. W. Bush was then in office and started another federal entity called the Resolution Trust Corp (RTC) to handle all the defunct S&Ls and the enormous portfolio of real estate properties, including apartments, condos, homes, office buildings, shopping centers, and warehouses. There was not one real estate market untouched.

I became an approved RTC contractor and started another new real estate company called TransCorp Realty to oversee and manage bank-foreclosed projects. I was 27 years old by then. I partnered with one of the richest men in Louisiana named Joe Canizaro. He and I were 50/50 partners and went on to manage and sell properties in Tyler, Texas, and Monroe, Louisiana. This included Glenwood Mall in Monroe and numerous other commercial projects in and around Tyler, Shreveport, and Monroe. As the economy began to recover, lending and commercial real estate were still very difficult, not only in Texas, but throughout the U.S. My parents by that point had moved from Dallas during the recession, to Miami, Florida, because Miami seemed to be recovering faster than any other area in the country.

Sometimes Obstacles Bring Success

Success does not come without its trials, though. It is important to remember that it is okay if your journey becomes difficult. Sometimes it's the world around you that is falling apart — in this case, the economy — and other times, it is a war within yourself. We may find ourselves feeling hindered due to our failures or struggles, but it is nothing about which to be ashamed. Honor these trials for what they are and learn to grow beyond them.

> *"All our dreams can come true if we have the courage to pursue them."*
> *— Walt Disney*

As you think of your goals and path in life, write down what your obstacles may be and ways in which you may overcome those obstacles. Think of those you know — business colleagues, friends, or family — who can help you reach your goals. Categorize those people into those who can support you emotionally and those with business connections or other relevant connections. And most importantly, always believe in yourself and never give up hope. After all, you are your own biggest obstacle. It doesn't matter how many people are cheering you on if you still don't believe in yourself.

I dare you to tell yourself or even write down, as frequently as you can, "I will achieve [insert your goal here]." Put together a Vision Board. Dream Big. It is all possible and within your reach.

> *"Who knows what miracles*
> *You can achieve*
> *(You can achieve)*
> *When you believe,*
> *somehow you will,*
> *You will when you believe."*
>
> *— Mariah Carey, When You Believe*

Songwriter: Stephen Schwartz
When You Believe lyrics © Universal Music Publishing Group

> *"Never be ashamed of a scar. It simply means you were stronger than whatever tried to hurt you."*
> — *Unknown*

life is not about waiting for the storm to pass its about learning to dance in the rain

— *Vivian Greene*

Chapter 5
MOVING ON

As I was finishing the sale of Glenwood Mall in West Monroe, my dad called and suggested we move to Florida. He said the recovery of commercial real estate and the state of the economy looked to be improving in Miami faster than Texas and Louisiana. At this time, my wife's brother Keith was a Thunderbird pilot with the Air Force, and the Thunderbirds were doing an air show in Tampa, Florida. We decided to drive to Tampa and see Keith and a live Thunderbird Air Show exhibition. It was spectacular! While in Tampa, we visited the beaches, including St. Pete Beach, and I suddenly realized — I can rebuild anywhere. So, why not build in the place where we love waking up?

Soon after, we moved to Florida and I got a job working for a large developer, building build-to-suit freestanding Eckerd Drug Stores. This was my first job where I did not work for myself. Eckerd Corporation was an American drug store chain that was headquartered in Largo, Florida and the oldest of the "big four" drugstore chains, founded in September of 1898 by 27-year-old J. Milton Eckerd and Z. Tatom in Erie, Pennsylvania. In the company's early years, it operated at 1105 State Street in downtown Erie as the Erie Cut-Rate Medicine Store. In 1912, Eckerd and Tatom sold their original store to Eckerd's sons and moved to Wilmington, Delaware, establishing a new store. From Delaware, the chain expanded to North Carolina and later to Florida. Jack Eckerd, son of the founder, was responsible for the expansion of the company when he acquired three stores in Florida in 1952.

The chain had approximately 2,800 stores in 23 states as far west as Arizona. In November 1996, Eckerd Drugs was purchased by J.C. Penney. Then, in April of 2004, the fourth largest drug chain in the U.S. was broken up in a $4.52 billion deal, with approximately 1,269 stores in Florida, Louisiana, and Texas. This included Eckerd's $1.3 billion mail order pharmacy, sold to CVS Corporation, now CVS Health. The deal enabled CVS to leapfrog past rival Walgreens with some 5,400 stores. Because CVS already owned 74 stores in Florida at the time, including 19 in the Tampa Bay area, many duplicate locations were closed. The remaining stores were sold to the Quebec-based Jean Coutu Group and merged with its Brooks Pharmacy chain. The Eckerd name and corporate headquarters, which housed 1,000 administrative workers at the time in Largo, Florida, would remain temporarily intact while under the Coutu ownership.

The sale erased the chain's name among its 622 Florida stores, where it had been synonymous with the pharmacy business since Jack Eckerd bought three old drugstores in the Tampa Bay area in 1952. Brooks Eckerd, Jean Coutu's U.S. operations would eventually be sold to Rite Aid. In return, a stake in Rite Aid was ceded to the French-Canadian company. The remaining Eckerd locations became Rite Aids.
(source: https://en.wikipedia.org/wiki/Eckerd_Corporation)

I worked for this company for 14 months and delivered 14 new freestanding Eckerd Drug Stores in that time. I put each site for Eckerd Drugs under contract, prepared the Pro-forma for Eckerd (cost of land and building cost together with permitting fees), and submitted back to Eckerd all the information for Eckerd Corp. Real Estate Committee to approve the site and the deal, as well as prepare a lease for the developer.

Just more than a year working with Eckerd, I quit the company and went back into business for myself. I started CDE Development, LLC, and CDE Enterprises, LLC. I went on to develop more than 40 projects totaling 100 million dollars in development. I was also a preferred developer for Starbucks, Outback, Chili's, Carrabba's, CVS, in addition to developing shopping centers, purchasing centers and an office building, including a Marriott Hotel. Then came 2008. Here we go again. Another recession. Would I make it through this one?

One by one, I had centers, mostly mom-and-pop tenants, who could no longer pay the rental rates. We also had several credit tenants who could not pay full rent. Many tenants were asking for a 50 percent rent reduction. This meant that I could not make my debt service, which is the amount of the mortgage payment plus expenses to keep the loan current, taxes, and insurance. When I started in the commercial real estate business, I was told, "The foundation and number one principle, is to never fall in love with a piece of property and only do credit tenant deals." I lost my direction and perspective. I sold most of the credit deals I developed before the recessions. I had one freestanding Starbucks, two freestanding Outbacks, one freestanding Carrabba's, and one freestanding Panera Bread. It seemed as if everything was falling apart when I had been so accustomed to everything falling into place.

As the economy got worse, cash became a premium. I had been trying to hold onto the centers that were draining all my cash and reserves. I had $3 million cash in the bank and ended up depleting all of it. In 2012, I had one shopping center located in Clearwater, Florida, that I started with a $5 million loan from First National Bank. FNB was declared insolvent by the FDIC, and another bank, called Stearns Bank, took over FNB. At that time, I had three tenants unable to pay full rent, and I was losing $15,000 a month. The mortgage payments were $35,000 a month.

Stearns Bank bought the assets of FNB at a fraction of the loan cost with TARP money from the Federal Government, but to me, they still showed the full loan of the $5 million that I owed Stearns Bank. The bank agreed to allow me to sell the center at a short sale for $1.8 million. A buyer was located for the $1.8 million, and the buyer funded the $1.8 million into a trust account, to which I was the sole trustee. But, because I had also placed the Clearwater Shopping Center in Chapter 11 bankruptcy, I had to wait on court approval to accept the $1.8 million. Until then, the $1.8 million sat in the trust account, and I looked at the $1.8 million daily for more than three weeks. At some point I thought that I could use a portion of those proceeds to pay other debts and return the money before it was missed. I found myself trying to justify my actions by paying $350,000 to my wife for the $500,000 Certificate of Deposit I had cashed a year before trying to save another shopping center called Van Dyke Commons, a 28-million-dollar center anchored with LA Fitness. Other tenants included Petland, Golfsmith, Home Goods, McDonald's, Regions Bank, Bank of America, Massage Envy, Dollar Tree, and Walgreens.

During this time frame, the banks were calling the loans due, knowing that there was no efficient market to refinance the centers. Most of the real estate loans were made through a construction loan then into a mini-perm loan, which was typically three years. At the end of three years, the loan could be renewed for additional points to the lender, could sell the center, or be refinanced with another bank. No one was lending between 2008 and 2010, and if they were, the terms were 60 percent LTV, loan to value. The problem was when the center was built it was an 80 to 90 percent LTV. At that point, I had to come up with a down payment of another one million dollars to get a new loan, when I could not save the center, too. The fear and panic continued inside of me, and all I could think about was saving my business, my marriage, my name, my reputation, yet I ended up losing it *all* with a series of bad choices. I cashed in a $500,000 CD to pay down the loan on Van Dyke and eventually lost that, too.

That's when I took $800,000 out of the trust account from the proceeds of the Clearwater Shopping Center.

I rationalized that I could put the money back in a few weeks when I sold a freestanding Starbucks I owned.

However, that did not happen.

When Stearns Bank called me and asked that I wire the $1.8 million to them, I wired one million and had to tell them that I took the $800,000 to pay another debt. Stearns Bank didn't wait around long before they asked the bankruptcy judge for an emergency hearing to inform the court that I took $800,000 from the trust account. I lied to the bank, to myself, and to my wife. There went vanity again. I had violated the trust of so many people.

I was so distraught that I kept my secret buried deep inside, not sharing with anyone until I had to show up in court. I had no choice but to tell the truth to the judge that I took the $800,000 from the trust account. The shame that consumed me was overwhelming.

I showed up in court with my attorney and told the truth. What else could I do? I knew I had made a mistake, and I knew I had to do the right thing. The judge ordered me to give my deposition to Stearns Bank and find out where I spent $800,000. I was to report back to the court. One week later, I still had not told my wife nor anyone else what was happening. The only person who knew was my attorney. I felt hopeless — how could I tell my wife? How could I tell anyone? It wasn't as if I had made a minor error, this was a criminal offense. The mere idea of confessing to my family filled me with terror and shame.

Giving Up

At the time, I owned a 42-foot Regal 4080 Sportyacht, named *Against All Odds*, and kept it for eight years at a covered slip marina in St. Petersburg. I thought the best and only way out was to commit suicide. It's a strange, solemn, and heartbreaking experience when you decide to take your own life. Without telling anyone, I went to my boat and brought enough over-the-counter pills to overdose. With four bottles of store-bought Tylenol and sleeping pills in hand, I arrived at my boat at 4 p.m. I wrote an "I'm sorry" suicide letter to my wife and kids, then took all the pills around 10 p.m. The rest is a blur of darkness and confusion before I was awakened by the dockmaster at the marina. He broke open the sliding door to the salon of the boat and came aboard where he found me passed out in the forward birth. I had vomited and could have choked on my own vomit, but for some reason, my life was interrupted by dockmaster Joe.

Not everyone in my position is so blessed to have such an interruption, but I am eternally grateful I did. The next few hours unfolded heartbreakingly so. And in a way, silently, because nobody knew what I had done.

Elaine had been calling me since 6 p.m. and was panicking when she called the marina and asked Joe to drive out to the dock and see if our black convertible T-Bird was in the parking lot, and if so, if there were any lights on in our boat. Joe went to the boat and told Elaine that my car was in the parking lot, and no lights were on inside the boat. Elaine told Joe to break the glass or door and do whatever it took to get inside to see if I was there. Since I had two heart attacks previously, she thought I could have had another heart attack. I was rushed to the hospital, and the emergency staff thought it was carbon monoxide poisoning, which is common on a boat. They ruled out a heart attack. I stayed in the hospital overnight, and Elaine stayed with me by my side, but I still couldn't tell her nor anyone else what had happened yet. If I had told her then, that meant I would have to come clean about everything. Like a child covering their eyes and believing the monster wasn't there, it seemed as if I didn't talk about the problem, maybe it would go away.

Secret Revealed

The very next day I went home and was asleep when around noon the doorbell rang, I rose to answer it and met a Deputy U.S. Marshal standing at the door waiting to arrest me for contempt of court. It all came crashing down at that moment.

The monster — my secret — was finally exposed, and there was no hiding any longer. Not only that, but it felt as if this was the beginning of the end. You can imagine how I was feeling — just days after a suicide attempt, hiding my mistake, and knowing I would likely go to prison. Looking back at the beginning of my story, I was that young boy who wanted to be a Cadillac owner, and a successful, intelligent businessman. What are the odds that I'd end up in this situation? Yet there I was. One choice, one terrible, terrible choice. That's all it took. It does not matter all the good you do in your life; all it takes is one bad choice or a series of bad choices, and all the good you did is erased.

But you will not be defined by your poor choices, it is what you do beyond that moment, that will define you. Stand tall, be humble, and don't be ashamed of your mistakes. God has a bigger plan and destiny for you, one that is imaginable.

At that point, I broke down and told my wife the truth of what I did and had been going through. I handed her the suicide letter that I had written, still in my pants pocket. No one checked my pants when I was rushed to the hospital. All my secrets were exposed.

My attorney said I would be charged with embezzlement or fraud, which is considered a white-collar crime. The FBI would file an indictment and prosecute the case since it involved a federal bank. White-collar crimes include bank fraud/mortgage fraud, insurance fraud, wire fraud, or embezzlement, are all usually felony offenses, punishable by jail or prison time, with substantial fines and other court sanctions. In addition to the criminal penalties, a conviction for fraud or theft is a black mark that may threaten professional licensure, business relationships, career paths, job opportunities, and one's reputation in the community.

This all happened in September 2012. It took four years for the FBI to indict me. These are not the odds I thought I'd be facing, and I wasn't sure if I'd overcome this trial or if somehow I'd survive *Against All Odds*.

My wife asked for a divorce a few months after the ordeal began in August 2012. We were divorced in January 2013 after 32 years of marriage. Another example of how life is a series of unexpected interruptions. Shortly after my divorce, I found myself experiencing such self-doubt, questioning all that I had done, and pleading with God.

> *"This burden is bigger than I can handle,*
> *I give it up to you God."*
> *— Clark East*

New Faith-filled Project

I was surfing on the internet for a positive, uplifting scripture or quote, and at that moment, I came up with the idea of a Faith Coin. This was something I could keep in my pocket, rub, or hold, and keep as a reminder that God loves me, and I am not alone. I tried searching for a coin or something else small to carry with me. I could not find anything, so I began searching the web for a company that made coins.

Clark's Custom Faith Coin

I found one, called them the next day, and told the gentleman over the phone of my idea, and he said they could manufacture the type of coin I wanted. I developed the wording and design and had 200 coins made. I gave them all out to friends, family, and strangers. I gave a coin to anyone who I felt at that moment needed it. I plan to have more made and do the same thing.

It may not seem like it, especially at that dark time in my life, but I had, and still have, a lot for which to be thankful. I found myself down, but not out by any means. My attitude was always, *never, never, never give up.*

While driving to Tallahassee for the weekend to visit my youngest son, Brendan, who was a freshman at the time at Florida State University, I experienced a revelation of sorts. About halfway through the drive, I threw my cigarette out the window of my 2008 Black Cadillac Escalade, turned the radio off and said, "God, whatever I am supposed to do, please show me the way. Guide me to what I need to be doing right now." I cried and turned to some soul music, which was, and still is, my favorite. I listened intently to those Motown classics as I waited to hear God's voice speak to me.

It was about 3 p.m. when I arrived in Tallahassee, and I went straight to Brendan's door. He was a Resident Assistant for his dorm, which meant he had his own dorm room. When I got there, he had just finished his chemistry labs and said he forgot his backpack in the chem lab and ran to see if it was still there. He had his laptop computer and cellphone in his backpack. When he returned with it, I asked him if that had happened to him before, and he said no, but it happened all over campus daily.

College students keep everything in their backpacks. There are 39,000 students at FSU alone. I thought of LSU with 42,000 students and every other college in the U.S. and abroad where the same thing occurs. Kids with backpacks that are misplaced, lost, or stolen.

After spending the weekend with Brendan, I spoke to my daughter Jamie as I headed back home to Clearwater. She asked if I heard the tragic news over the weekend about a nine-year-old who was kidnapped by a child molester in front of a Walmart in Jacksonville. Tragically, she was found raped and dead nine hours later, still with her bicycle helmet on. I got home Sunday night and sat on my computer and started searching Google for tracking devices.

Seek and You Shall Find

I did not find anything that completed the entire cycle of the moment that when an item is on the move, you could be alerted or notified and then capture in real-time a tracking system that showed every move of the item. That's when I came up with the idea of TracFind, which alerts police at the sole discretion of the consumer.

The next day I called our local sheriff, Sheriff Gee of Hillsborough County. I knew him personally, since I was an honorary sheriff; I even had a badge and did the training for eight years. I told Sheriff Gee of my idea, but also included guns. I said, "Sheriff if I could invent a GPS tracking device small enough to be hidden in a gun, bicycle helmet, TV, etc. — what do you think?"

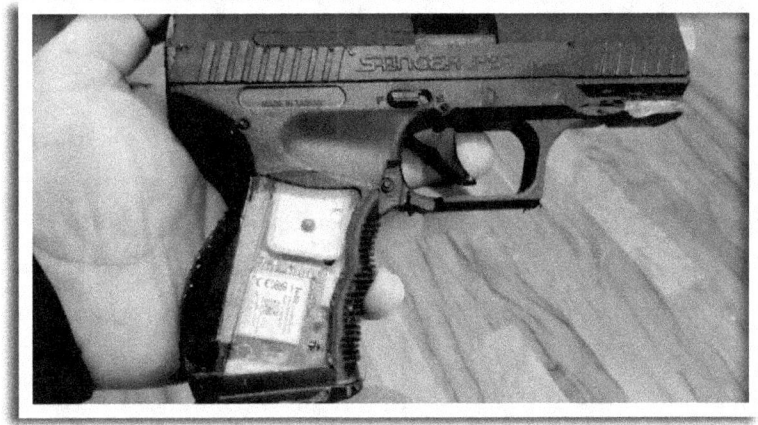

Example of TracFind inside a gun

He said if I could get one for the gun industry, I would need to get around civil liberties, so whatever I invented could not invade civil liberties. It would have to be at the sole discretion of the consumer. I started on my journey to find a solution. If I were a parent of a college student, would I want a GPS device to track my child's backpack, my child, my parent with dementia, my gun, bicycle, motorcycle, TV, or anything of value for that matter? I was on the internet and started to Google software and hardware companies. The overall theme was, "If you can dream it, we can build it."

There are storms in our lives where it seems there is no end, no light at the end of the tunnel, and the only option is to give up. Giving up presents itself in many ways: suicide, addiction, isolation, and the overall consuming emotion of hopelessness. Once you lose hope, that's the moment you give up. It's okay to lose hope for a brief moment — I did.

Remember, though, that whatever you are facing will pass, just like all the trials you faced before.

Even this, even these dark times in my life, transformed from a hopeless reality to memory. My story wasn't quite over yet. Neither is yours. Keep pushing yourself forward. Your story doesn't need to be graceful, oftentimes surviving is messy. All that matters is that you don't give up. I *wanted* to give up. I *tried* to give up. Be it God or the Universe, I wasn't given the option. I was saved from my attempt, and it is my prayer that you never sink that low. My greatest piece of advice is to not let fear and hopelessness consume you. I let fear drive many of my choices those days, and you see where it led me.

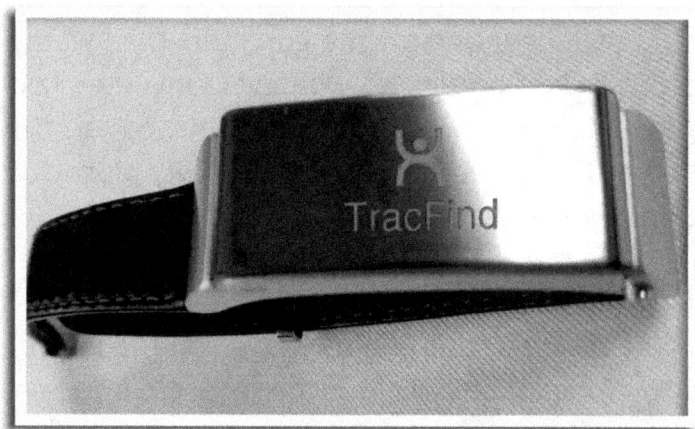

I was awarded a U.S. Patent on my invention on June 13, 2017, however, because of my conviction and poor choices that led to my incarceration, TracFind came to a halt. I'm now working to bring it back to life.

If you're currently in the storm, unable to see the light, I challenge you to empower yourself with the knowledge that you have the ability to overcome anything. Envision where you want to be, no matter how far off it may seem. It may even help to imagine the little steps that will take you to your destination.

> *"You're about to overcome something you have been dealing with. Your mind and soul will soon be at peace again. Be patient. Everything will be okay!*
> *—Unknown*

Think of the hardest thing you've ever been through. Remember how you thought you wouldn't get through it? But you did, right? You're reading this book, and that proves that you still have a lot more fight left in you. Everything is going to be okay... you only must believe it, even if all you can believe is that one day it will work out.

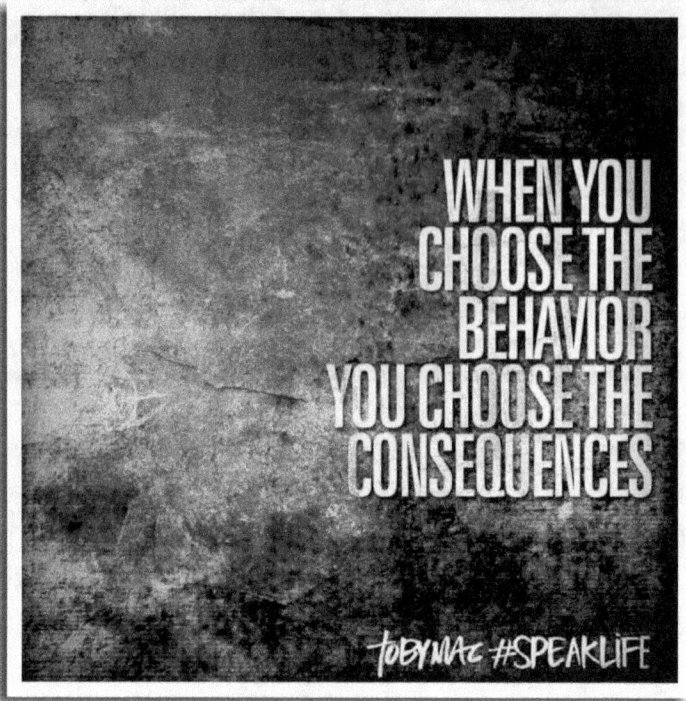

> "My philosophy is to kill the monster while it's little. The best time to handle a negative emotion is when you first begin to feel it. It's much more difficult to interrupt an emotional pattern once it's full-blown."
> — Tony Robbins

Chapter 6
INTERRUPTED

Life is a series of unexpected interruptions.

On December 4, 2016, I was indicted and arrested by the FBI. I was sentenced to 30 months in federal prison.

Prior to my demise, I had it all. I was married for 32 years. Had a beautiful 4,200-square-foot, Colonial-style, two-story home with a pool. I lived in that home for 15 years until I moved to Houston in 2016. I had several boats, two Cadillacs, several Escalades, a T-Bird, a Corvette, and everything that I thought represented success. I equated my self-worth to my net worth. I was too prideful to recognize earlier that the things I so desperately tried to protect were not at all or even close to what is precious in my world: love, life, and family. Nothing can replace family and love. Material things are just *things*. They mean zero when faced with the loss of love and family, and ultimately, freedom.

> *"The rich invest in time; the poor invest in money."*
> — *Warren Buffett*

Being a real estate developer afforded me an affluent lifestyle. My estimated net worth was more than $50 million, and at one time as high as $80 million, with more than $3 million cash in the bank. Affluent is one way to put it. My home in Clearwater was worth more than $850,000 at one time. I could have paid off the mortgage yet continued to leverage cash and assets to keep building my development. I had all the trappings of a first-rate multi-millionaire with room to grow. I bought my dad a Cadillac convertible, as well as matching Rolex Blue/Silver Datejust watches. My youngest son went to private prep school costing $15,000 per year. His high school senior year cost more than $20,000 alone! He earned an academic scholarship to Florida State and a full scholarship to Washington University for a master's in social work in 2018. Needless to say, my son was totally devastated when he found out what I had done. We previously afforded him a stay in France to study abroad, and he became a successful clinical social worker for a major medical hospital in Denver, Colorado.

We had money to spend. We had money to spare. Elaine went to Europe while the kids went everywhere they wanted. I stayed behind and worked. In hindsight I should have invested more time in my family. The ROI was much higher, but I couldn't see it at that time. We would routinely write $1,000 to $2,500 checks to conservative causes, pet projects, fundraisers, paid cash for most things, as well as gifted money to kids and parents, including a $60,000 gift to our son to a buy home.

> *"If money is the only problem you have, then friend you don't have problems."*
> *— Unknown*

Chapter 7
FLORIDA SPORTS HALL OF FAME

I had the honor of serving on the board of the Florida Sports Hall of Fame from 2008 through 2012, where I rubbed shoulders with historic and famous ball players like Pat Summerall, Jack Hall, Emmitt Smith, Burt Reynolds, and others. It was a traumatic phone call for me to the president, Rick Dantzler, to tell him I was stepping down, and to confess that I was stepping down to avoid a public relations problem because of my troubles. I told him that I didn't want to embarrass the board and would rather step down then. Rick said that he appreciated my work and dedication to the board and that I would always have a seat whenever I wanted to return.

One of my favorite memories during my tenure on the board of the Florida Sports Hall of Fame, was inducting Lee Corso, class of 2003, who was an American sports broadcaster and football analyst for ESPN, as well as a former coach. He has been a featured analyst on ESPN's College GameDay program since its inception in 1987. Mr. Corso served as the head football coach at the University of Louisville from 1969 to 1972, at Indiana University Bloomington from 1973 to 1982, and at Northern Illinois University in 1984, compiling a career college football coaching record of 73-85-6. He was the head coach for the Orlando Renegades of the United States Football League in 1985, tallying a mark of 5-13. He attended Florida State and Miami Jackson Senior High.

Lee Corso on the left, Florida Sports Hall of Fame inductee and Burt Reynold's roommate while at FSU

It was our practice to call inductees to ask who they would like to have introduce them on the stage, he asked for Burt Reynolds, since they went to school together. He gave me his information, so I called Burt and he agreed, but only on a few provisos: 1) that he be picked up in a private jet; 2) to be given the tail number of the jet; and 3) to know the name of the pilot.

At first, I thought it was a little strange, but he told me that he needs to check the safety and maintenance records of the aircraft and a background check on the pilot to make sure the flight would be safe.

Clark and Burt Reynolds flying into Tampa from his private air strip in Jupiter, Florida

I was fortunate to borrow a plane from an FSU alumni friend of another board member, Barry Smith. Barry was a former wide receiver in the National Football League who played 42 games for the Green Bay Packers. Smith played one season with the Tampa Bay Buccaneers and retired from the NFL in 1976. So, once everything had cleared, I had the pleasure of boarding the plane in Tampa, then went on to Jupiter to pick up Burt for an entertaining 45-minute flight back. Burt was everything that was said about the guy. He was down to earth with a big heart and an even bigger laugh.

Of course, I asked Burt what his favorite movie was, and he told me that of all the movies he made, *The Longest Yard* was his favorite. "We really played a game of football that day," he said recalling the filming on location at Georgia State Prison in Reidsville, Georgia. The production had the cooperation of then-Governor, Jimmy Carter. Filming had to be delayed from time to time due to prison uprisings. Burt reminisced a little as a running back for the Seminoles during his college years in the late 1950s when he and Lee were teammates and remained close friends for life.

Burt told me that the movie he will always be remembered for is *Smoky and the Bandit*.

> *Car enthusiasts no doubt would recognize Burt Reynolds from his starring role in Smokey and the Bandit, where he played the lovable outlaw Bo Darville, a bootlegger who distracts police in a Pontiac Trans Am. The Bandit-style Pontiac Trans Am sold at auction for $172,000.*

"It was the first movie ever made where the car had a leading role," Burt said. "Let me tell you something," he led forward. "That movie sold more Pontiac Trans Ams than any dealership GM had at the time. The president of GM told me that I was responsible for sales skyrocketing more than 300 percent and he would like to send me a free Trans Am each year for life!

"And so, for the next six years, each year in January, I would see this 18-wheeler drive up and drop off a brand-new Trans Am," he said. "I started gifting the cars to friends and family or donating to a local hospital to raise money.

"But then January of the seventh year came around and no 18-wheeler, no car. I waited a few months, then called the president's office to learn that he had a heart attack and wasn't available.

"A month rolls by, and the new president of GM calls me and tells me that sales dropped sharply, and they were no longer in the position to honor his predecessor's promise.

"The lesson is that when someone promises you something for life, ask them if they mean your life... or theirs!" Burt said with a big laugh. He never got a Trans Am for himself. Burt Reynolds passed away in September of 2018, leaving behind an impressive resume filled to bursting with box-office hits.

> *"If someone promises you something for life, ask if they meant your life or theirs."*
> *— Burt Reynolds*

I met a lot of other famous ball players, politicians, heads of state, entertainers like Emmitt Smith, Dan Marino, Wade Boggs, President Bush, and others.

George Allen "Pat" Summerall (May 10, 1930 – April 16, 2013) was an American football player and television sportscaster who worked for CBS, Fox, and ESPN. In addition to football, he also announced major golf and tennis events. In total, he announced 16 Super Bowls on network television (more than any other announcer), 26 Masters Tournaments, and 21 U.S. Opens. He also contributed to 10 Super Bowl broadcasts on CBS Radio as a pregame host or analyst.

Florida Sports Hall of Fame event with Pat Summerall

Pat Summerall got his job when he answered the phone bank in college. Mr. Summerall played football for the Arkansas Razorbacks. A journalist on the other end of the phone wanted to talk to one of the players. Mr. Summerall said that he would try and find him. The journalist told him that he had a natural broadcast voice and asked if he would like to test for radio. The rest is history, I guess. Mr. Summerall was inducted into the Florida Sports Hall of Fame because in high school he played football for Columbia in Lake City, Florida.

> *"When someone saves your life, and gives you life, there's gratitude, humility; there's a time you've been so blessed you realize you've been given another chance at life that maybe you did or didn't deserve."*
>
> *— Pat Summeral*

Florida Sports Hall of Fame with Emmett Smith of the Dallas Cowboys

One of the inductees I had the honor of meeting while I was a board member, was Louis Victor Piniella, Class of 1977, who was born in Tampa on August 25, 1943. He attended Jesuit High School of Tampa where he was an All-American in basketball. For college, he attended the University of Tampa where he was an All-American in baseball. Lou Piniella told me of the day he was drafted into the Yankees. He said that usually the player finds his name on his locker with his uniform hung up waiting for him, but on his first day with the Yankees, his name was not on his locker and there was no sign of a uniform. He was sent to Steinbrenner's office and was told that until he could walk on water his hair will be cut short. He left to get a haircut and when he returned, his uniform and name were on his locker.

George Steinbrenner and Lou Piniella during a 1987 chat. [Times files]

Clark had the pleasure of meeting both George Steinbrenner and Lou Piniella and ended up buying a Marriott Fairfield from the Steinbrenner family in 2010

I would say that 99 percent of inductees thanked their father or a coach from little league or high school. I never heard any of them thank their realtor, financial broker, or even their personal banker.

A Presidential Meeting

My dad and I had the pleasure meeting President George W. Bush. After a few years of donating to the RNC, I got a phone call telling me that President George W. Bush was hosting a presidential dinner/gala event and I was invited to attend to meet President Bush who wanted to thank me in person for my contributions.

Clark, President George W. Bush, and Douglas East

if someone contributes consistently to the National Republican Committee, they'll get an invite to meet the president. Mine came in an embossed, gold-sealed letter to meet the president. The invite cost $12,500 per person, $25,000 for two people to meet President George W. Bush. Since I already had taken Elaine, she suggested I take Dad.

I called Dad and asked, "What are you doing March 6th? Would you like to meet the president?" And for one short minute my dad was a kid again.

We filled out paperwork for the Secret Service and before you knew it, we had checked into the Hilton. Our meeting was at 4 p.m., but Dad was dressed and ready to go by noon. He was really excited. We were told to be there an hour early. It was just me and Dad with the Secret Service all around. We met the Secret Service sunglasses, holding a clipboard, and checked in and were told to "stand here, the president's on his way." We were wanded, scanned, patted, and combed, then ushered into a side room to wait for the president.

Dad and I were standing in the middle of a little room exchanging small talk when a hand reached through and pulled back the curtain and President Bush stepped through with an extended hand and smile, and said, "Hi, pleasure to meet you," as he put his hands around both of us as the photographer snapped our picture. He asked if we knew his brother, "I understand you are from Florida, in construction and development."

I said, "Thank you for protecting our country."

He replied, "I couldn't do it with without God."

He said he loved a father and son team and he talked to his dad daily. From there we went to a formal dinner and sat beside Trace Adkins and Adam Putnam, Florida's Commissioner of Agriculture. That night we met Newt Gingrich and Carl Rove. There were only about 100 people in the room and President Bush was no more than 10 feet away.

Two minutes is a *very* long time with the president of the United States. Dad was over the moon.

The Darkest Hour

"Dear God, I'm not really sure you're even listening right now. It certainly doesn't seem like it. I'm done. I can't do this anymore. If you want it done, you must do it. Whatever you are doing with me, get it over with, because this hurts too much.

"I'm angry, and I'm pretty sure I'm angry with you. I don't understand. I feel like you've turned your head and you don't see me anymore, you're not listening, and you don't care. Everything I've ever learned about you says you are kind and loving and you want the best for me, and I'd like to believe that, but I can't seem to bring myself to risk it. If I believe that, then it means that the hell I am living through right now is somehow for my good. I want something else. Not this.

"So, if you are who and what you say you are, and if you really do care about me and you really do hear me, then... I don't know... do something. Show up. Give me something to work with. I'm tired of hurting, and I am utterly helpless. You're all I really have, and I'm scared you're not there. Amen."

The Prayer from the Darkest Hour
September 25, 2011
by Jonathan Hart, LPC

CLARK EAST

Chapter 8
LOOKING INWARD — UPWARD

When I was in my darkest moments, I prayed to God, it doesn't matter who your God is nor where your faith may be at any time in your life or anywhere along your journey. When you find yourself in despair or in a dark place and feeling completely alone, stop, breathe, and pray. Pray to God or the universe, a loved one, a power greater than yourself, reach out to that strength and hold on. Your best days are yet to come. Everyone has a story to share, an event that took place in your life that led you in a direction or down a chosen path. It is like driving and the directions offer you one route, street, road, or even an alternate path. The road you choose often is what leads to a whole new destination, place, or person you would not ordinarily have met.

My purpose in writing this book is to let readers know that falling in life is not a failure. The road less traveled, although it may be safer at times, is not where life's journeys develop. I choose to believe that it's the most populated roads in life that can be the most complicated and the most rewarding, because you never know who you may meet along the way.

The miracle, the change of events, the new direction, or the beginning — the unexpected interruption shapes your life. I am inspired by stories of Ray Croc the founder of McDonald's who, at the age of 51, was selling milkshake machines and then founded the McDonald Brothers Hamburger restaurant and had that vision when everyone around him thought he was crazy for dreaming big, thinking big, and visualizing that he could franchise McDonald's around the U.S. and beyond. Thomas Edison failed more than 1,000 times before he finally created a successful light bulb. No one who has achieved big or small in business, love, or whatever they were pursuing, succeeded on the first try. It is during unexpected experiences when an idea comes to mind, a change is made in your heart, or determination fuels your drive.

When I was meeting with several big business figures to talk about my invention, TracFind, I was amazed by story after story of how so many great companies were started. All, just like myself, were encountering Mr. Ross Perot's in-house and personal attorney and CPA Mike Poss. He told me that Bill Gates approached Ross Perot not long after he sold his company, Electronic Data Systems, and asked him to invest in his new company, Microsoft. Mr. Perot did not see the merits in Microsoft, he elected to pass on the investment.

Then Steve Jobs from Apple went to Mr. Perot and he invested 20 million with Steve Jobs. There's no telling what that return is today!

Another startup gentleman approached Mr. Perot, named Arthur Blank. Mr. Blank presented Mr. Perot with a business plan to open a hardware lumber company the size of Walmart. Mr. Perot could not see hardware stores that large and passed on investing with Mr. Blank. Arthur Blank founded Home Depot, and today with his co-founder is worth 200 billion. Mr. Blank also owns the Atlanta Falcons NFL. Those are just a few examples of success, some of which occurred despite rejections.

> *"Dear God,*
> *Thank you that ALL work has significance because work is good. Help me bring you glory today, through my actions, my words, through the good work I do to bring order to my little corner of the world."*
> — Amen

Inmate Job Opportunity

Each part of this journey continues to open doors that I never expected while I was incarcerated at Three Rivers Federal Prison camp in Three Rivers, Texas.

I was given a job as the tool clerk at camp maintenance. The tool clerk job entailed being responsible for all maintenance tools for HVAC (Heating & Air Conditioning), electrical, and plumbing at the prison camp. The tool clerk room had three walls with a template outline of every tool, including: pliers, screwdrivers, drills, hammers, skill saws, etc.

When an approved skilled inmate came to the tool room, I would check out a specific tool or tools to the inmate who was the plumber or electrician for a repair job at the camp, as an example. When a tool was given out, I would put a chip on the tooth which was pre-assigned to the inmate, so I knew at all times who had that particular tool checked out.

The inmate would then return the tool, and it was put back in its correct place, and the inmate's chip was removed off the wall.

There was always complete accountability if an inmate lost a tool. The inmate had to find the tool, or he would go to the *shoe* — a nickname for the medium lockdown single-cell unit and remain in lockdown for a week. It was serious for a tool to be missing. The entire camp would go on lockdown until a tool was found. Thankfully, it never happened on my watch, nor the entire three months I was in charge of the tool room.

My sweet mom would come visit me every two weeks in the Beaumont Camp during the 16 months that I was there. She was heartbroken for my troubles and only wanted to save her child and make the pain go away. Up until the day my dad died, he would say, "Son, they may take a piece of your ass, but they could never take your mind." He never judged me and always supported me. It was pure love. My father passed away March 5, 2016, before my incarceration.

Clark and his mother Bonnie East at the Beaumont Federal Prison Camp

> *"You'll find people who truly love you and true friends and family. You'll know who's not."*
> *— Author Unknown*

Chapter 9
RESIDENTIAL DRUG ABUSE PROGRAM (RDAP)

The Residential Drug Abuse Program (RDAP) is an intensive nine-month, 500-hour, substance-abuse rehabilitation program administered by the United States Federal Bureau of Prisons (BOP), offered to federal prisoners who qualify and voluntarily elect to enroll. Upon successful completion of the program, prisoners who meet the necessary criteria, are eligible for up to a 12-month reduction of their sentence and possibly six months in a halfway house depending on how many months are left on their sentence.

Due to the high demand and insufficient spots, inmates are placed on a waiting list typically when they have 12 months or less left to their sentence and are accepted when there is an opening. This is part of the reason why inmates receive different amounts of time off their sentences. For example, if an inmate has waited for a slot until he has 12 months left and the program is six months long, then he only receives six months off his sentence and so forth.

Violent offenses normally disqualify defendants from the early release portion of the program. Felony or misdemeanor convictions for homicide, forcible rape, robbery, aggravated assault, and child sexual abuses, all render a prisoner ineligible to participate. Bad behavior and regular rule breaking will definitely lead to expulsion from the Residential Drug Abuse Program.

When I learned about RDAP, I first thought it didn't really apply to me. The program is open to inmates with a documented history of substance abuse in the 12-month period prior to arrest for the sentence they are currently serving. It is authorized in 18 U.S.C. § 3621. RDAP is only available to inmates in federal prisons; state prisoners are not eligible to participate.

I spoke to my lawyer who wrote a letter to the judge explaining my addiction and how RDAP would help turn my life around. The BOP shows lower rates of recidivism and a higher quality of life upon returning to civilian life for offenders who successfully complete the program. I had a drinking problem to push away the shame and guilt, so I qualified. if I successfully completed the program, I would shave a year off my sentence, I had a three-year sentence, no gun charge, and no violence. That's what allowed me to transfer from Three Rivers to Beaumont.

My first thought was that my sentence would be reduced. I never thought it would change my behavior nor my thinking. I was still trying to justify what I did but came to the conclusion that wrong was wrong. I did wrong. I did this for myself, not for anyone else. Nothing is worth the loss of freedom, integrity, and self-worth. Losing false friends wasn't a big issue. A true friend would not have turned their backs, good to know early on.

The feeling is the same, whether you rob a bank, or are a drug dealer — any crime is a crime. You have that same feeling. You lose everything: money, life, and marriage. You must know how to get back up and rebuild yourself, don't let your mistake define you. Learn and quickly get back up. Your opportunities will continue to make their way around until you're ready for them.

> *"Success is the ability to go from one failure to another without the loss of enthusiasm and trying and trying again to succeed, never, never, never to give up."*
> *— Winston Churchill*

What is divinely meant for you has no expiration date. Your chances aren't running or slipping away. Don't let the illusion of time work against you. You're exactly where you need to be, doing exactly what you should be doing. There is a purpose for every stage of life. Find comfort in that and continue pressing forward in peace.

RDAP was the turning point of my poor pitiful life. I never stopped to think about what I did to my wife, partners, kids, banks, and everyone else in my life. You try to justify your actions, but at the end of the day, you're still doing something wrong. RDAP made me realize that there's no justification for what I did.

A thing about mollification, I projected that things were worse than what they really were. The reality was that all I had to do was hand in the keys to the bank and go through bankruptcy, instead I thought I would look like a moron. Whatever you *think* is bad, is probably not as bad as you think. Face your fear, no matter what. As soon as you face your fear, it's over. There may still be consequences for your actions, but the fear is gone.

As I was losing money, I tied money to my self-worth, and it was hard to face, because of my lifestyle. **Change your thinking and you will change your results.** I don't need material things, my home doesn't define me, my bank account doesn't define me.

> *"Money is only a tool. It will take you wherever you wish, but it will not replace you as the driver."*
> *—Ayn Rand*

One bad result and society will never forget nor forgive you for the rest of your life.

My wife couldn't forgive me. If you're honest with yourself, people will respect that. Once you lose that trust, it's very difficult for people to trust you again.

When you are released from prison, there will still be people who will never accept you. These aren't the people you need in your life to begin with. You should never give up on yourself. If you don't believe in yourself, no one else will either.

Find that something to hang onto and climb back up that ladder, it's not how hard your fall, but how quickly you get back up that makes all the difference.

I don't need acceptance from people today, I know who I am. I am a guy who made a mistake. I quit believing in myself. RDAP taught me that God has a greater purpose for me and that until I get over myself, I'll never see what the purpose is.

There's nothing I can't overcome. I don't need anything nor any dollar sign to replace the love someone has for me.

> *"There is no defeat except from within, no really insurmountable barrier saves our own inherent weakness of purpose."*
> *—Elbert Green Hubbard*

CLARK EAST

Chapter 10
TURNING POINT

No matter what life brings your way, take the learning experiences as a disguised blessing. The journey you are on will reveal your purpose. Success is defined only by you and those who love you and know your heart, not money nor things. Finding what gives you peace, happiness, and unconditional love is success. The money and things you may acquire along the way are just the by-products of your success.

> *"Remember that your real wealth can be measured not by what you have, but by what you are."*
> —*Napoleon Hill*

Oliver Napoleon Hill, born on October 26, 1883, was an American self-help author. He is best known for his book *Think and Grow Rich*, published in 1937, which remains among the top 10 bestselling self-help books of all time. Hill's works insisted that fervid expectations are essential to improving one's life. Most of his books were promoted as expounding principles to achieve success.

Which of life's unexpected interruptions propelled you to become the person you are today? Did you ever think the reason something happened to you was to make something better in your future? The good that comes out of the bad things that happen to you is to help you become the best, better you, the person God created and intended for you to be. It's the *unexpected interruption* in life that places you where you need to be. Things happen to help you unload baggage or the parts of your life that were not helpful to you, and/or that were hurting you. It was recurring decisions and habits that kept me in the same place. I had to get off the treadmill. It took a major interruption to get my attention.

Interruptions in life ultimately help you discover who you really are. We go along thinking we know who we are until that event shakes our world and makes us realize that it needed to change, and we could not make that change until that moment. I now have a different meaning of cause and effect, and it's the first time in my life that this discovery of myself is allowing me to understand why I have made certain choices and how I can learn to make better choices. I believe that a life of satisfaction, meaning, and joy awaits us by simply re-focusing on putting God first and not asking God for things; nor to save me from a disaster. I learned, grew, and became the person God saw in me all along. Would the real YOU please stand up? Elaine said to me when all this happened, "Will the real Clark East please stand up?"

The following is another example of life's unexpected interruption. An inmate named Jonathan Smith, 41 and married with kids, lived directly behind me in my unit. Every day he would say, "Good morning, Mr. East." He was such a kind spirit, he had a wonderful smile, heart, and soul. He passed away while serving his sentence. He was jogging on the track and just dropped dead. Inmates tried giving him CPR, and then camp nurses tried to save him as well. We were told he passed away a few minutes after he fell. It's another unexpected interruption of life and death that can change in minutes. I only knew this man for three weeks, but

I was impacted and saddened by his death. What made his death feel real was when the correctional officer went to his locker located right behind me and cleaned out all his personal items. Only God knows why someone is taken from the earth so quickly. Take nothing for granted. Tell your loved ones you love them. Tell them you are sorry. Ask them to forgive you. Above all, let them feel your heart, your gratitude, and that your love is everlasting for them. Love is greater than anything on this earth. I want the last thing any of my loved ones hear from me to be, "I love you."

> *"If you are successful, remember that somewhere someone who loved you gave you a lift or an idea that started you in the right direction after your defeat. You are never defeated when you keep trying."*
> *—Napoleon Hill*

What I also learned is that if you **change your thinking, you will change your results**; the better choices I made, the better results I got. I also learned that the poor choices I made were out of fear, and I continued to justify those poor choices. It really was selfish on my part, I never realized just how selfish since at the time I could only think of myself. I was thinking of how it was going to affect *me*. I never stopped to think of the consequences, and certainly now to be able to reflect back and take account, not only accountability for my actions, but to take account of the choices I made, it brought to light that my choices truly affected so many people around me.

When Elaine asked, "How could I have made that choice?" All I kept thinking was, *wait you don't understand. I was only focused on me, me, me.* Little did I know. What I learned from this journey is that with any challenge I have in life, all I need to do is stop, breathe, and back up.

I can now ask, "Are the consequences worth the choices I'm getting ready to make?" If only I could have looked at myself in the mirror and said okay, these are the consequences of taking money that doesn't belong to me: I could be arrested, indicted, damage my reputation, destroy my marriage, lose my wife's respect, and that of my kids, and my business partners. In fact, I could lose a part of *me*. I could lose financially; I could go broke. I will violate the trust of so many.

Certainly, if I had been thinking clearly and rationally, I would have thought no way are those consequences worth taking money, it's just not, and certainly the consequences of losing freedom and going to prison. No way.

So, now I can truly address the fact that fear is not going to lead me in the future, it's not leading me today, it's not going to lead me tomorrow. Whatever difficult situation you may find yourself in, usually it's not as difficult as you think to overcome. You can get through it.

Stop. Breathe. Talk to someone. Communicate. I held everything in. I was so full of pride. I didn't want to share any of my mistakes with anyone. I didn't want to admit my vulnerability.

When I look back now, I thank God. I thank Him for saving me, "Thank You God for giving me a second chance. Thank You for allowing me to really look at myself." And as my youngest son Brendan would say, like his mom did, "Dad, would the real Clark East, please stand up?"

Another good friend said, "You know, Clark, God did not leave you. I did not leave you. You left God, and you left me."

> *"Fake friends like to see you do well...*
> *not better than them."*
> *–Author Unknown*

And that's so true for me and my statement. I was so wrapped up and only thinking of myself, not thinking of others and the bad choices I had made, that if I had simply stopped and communicated and had the courage to face that fear early on, I would have avoided all those difficulties. But it's through difficulties that we grow, it's through difficulties that we learn. It's certainly made me a better person. I hope I can share my story. Even if I just touch one life and save one person from going through what I did, by encouraging them to stop, back up, and breathe, I will be satisfied. I truly think that we're not alone. God is with us, even if you feel like you're the only person on the earth who understands what you're going through. God understands. Reach out, grab onto anything you can, and pick yourself back up again, because God is right there with you. Always remember to help someone, just as you were helped.

> *"You realize that without overcoming those*
> *obstacles, you would never have realized your*
> *potential, strength, will power, of heart."*
> *— Unknown*

Prayer for Seekers of Salvation

*Jesus, why would You die for me?
That is the hardest question I ask when
I come close to asking You into my heart
and taking Your free gift of grace.
How could You love me?*

*Yet, Jesus, I have read how You loved
David even when he committed adultery
and first-degree murder. I have done worse!
You loved Saul when he was terrorizing Christians,
and You turned him into someone valuable.*

*I long to be of value to someone. I have
abandoned my children, I have let my
parents down, and I have let You down.
But no more! Today, I commit to You and
accept Your free gift—Your grace—for me.
Thank You for loving me so much
that You would die for me.
As I speak these words, my spirit lifts.
I feel Your presence and the
power of the Holy Spirit coming over me.
Thank You, Jesus.*

Amen.

†

A prayer from the Inmate Devotional, "Doing His Time."

Chapter 11
THREE RIVERS

Before I share my last few words of wisdom and advice, I want to share my experience in prison. It's not a time to be glossed over, and I found that even this unexpected interruption brought so much insight and purpose into my life. As I mentioned, I was sentenced to 30 months in a federal prison camp. I self-surrendered, accepting whatever punishment would come my way.

> *"Jails and state prisons are the complement of schools; so many less as you have the latter, so many more you must have of the former."*
> —Horace Mann

At Three Rivers camp, where I stayed for three months until I was accepted into RDAP, I was called into the counselor's office and told that I would be leaving on a bus and transferred to the federal prison transfer station in Oklahoma City. I was awakened at 5 a.m. by an officer who said to follow him, as I would be boarding the bus. I was told that since I was a camper, I could be a trustee on the bus and not have to be shackled in handcuffs and leg chains. I thought I had won the lottery.

As soon as I got to the front of the bus, the guard on the bus pulled me to the side and confirmed that I would be a trustee on the bus for the 13-hour bus ride from Three Rivers, Texas, to Oklahoma City. During the bus ride, there were two armed guards with shotguns, one sat in the front of the bus and one at the rear of the bus. All the other inmates were shackled with handcuffs and chains on their feet. But my handcuffs were taken off, and I was able to hand out bag lunches to the other inmates on the bus and pick up the trash during the ride. The 13-hour bus ride was a journey in and of itself. All the windows had bars on them and were blacked out.

The bus was like a Greyhound bus, but totally gutted with a fence separating the bus driver and two guards sitting inside the fence with shotguns. Each time we stopped for gas during the journey, both guards would exit the bus and stand outside with their shotguns, making sure no one came around the bus. When we arrived at the Federal Detention Center in Oklahoma City later that night, we were escorted off the bus and led to an area where we stripped down naked and were given a new issue of inmate clothing. Then our names were called, one by one.

We then were escorted by guards to a particular floor at the Federal Detention Center. I was brought to the fifth floor. As soon as I walked off the elevator into the holding arena, I had my first look at a real prison setting. They took my handcuffs off and the shackles off my feet. I was led into the cell block on the fifth floor, where there were approximately 100 other men. I then was led to a two-person cell.

My cellmate was going to federal prison for a 10-year sentence for robbing a bank. The Federal Detention Center housed murderers, drug dealers, bank robbers, and white-collar crime inmates. We were all together in the general population. I would remain at the Federal Detention Center for two weeks until the day I was awakened at 5 a.m.

Again, I was placed in handcuffs and shackles, then led to another part of the five-story office building where a plane was waiting on the tarmac, also known as Con Air.

It truly resembled the plane that was in the movie Con Air. There were armed guards with shotguns, and all the inmates were in handcuffs and shackles. I was led to a seat and waited for the flight to Beaumont, Texas, to be transferred to the Beaumont camp, where I would enter into the Residential Drug and Alcohol Treatment Program. The plane ride was very quiet. No one spoke to anyone as the guards walked up and down the aisle with their shotguns.

When the plane landed in Beaumont, each inmate was escorted off the plane. There were several buses parked on the tarmac. The officer would call out names and tell the inmate which bus to board. As soon as I boarded the bus, I took a seat with a sigh of relief that finally, this part of the journey would be over soon, and the handcuffs would come off. I believed I would be in the camp setting again with as much freedom as a camp environment allows. Almost as soon as I sat down on the bus, a guard called my name and said, "East off the bus." My heart was pounding. I was full of fear. How could I be called off the bus? What was happening? Where was I going to go now? The uncertainty rattled me.

The guard said that the bus was full. They took three other inmates with me off the bus and had us re-board the plane and fly back to Oklahoma City to the Federal Detention

Center lockup. It didn't make any sense, but what choice did I have?

Apparently, the bus could not accommodate all the inmates. And because two other inmates and I were going to the camp, I guess that meant that we could be delayed, while the other prisoners were going to maximum lockup. It was a very scary time with the unknown and uncertainty. I kept asking myself questions that only led to even more fear. *Had there been a mistake? Did they get my file mixed up?* Feeling hopeless and frightened, I did the only thing I could. I said a prayer to God. I said, "God, please take care of me. Protect me. Watch over me. Help me get through this next phase." Sure enough, I boarded the plane and flew back to Oklahoma City, where I stayed another week and had to repeat the same procedures of stripping down to the nude bending over guards. It was the procedure to check your body to make sure you had no contraband or weapons. Then being escorted to another room to grab new prison clothing, one pillow, one blanket, and one sheet. I then was escorted back to the fifth floor, exactly where I was previously, along with the same inmates I had left.

That same morning, my only comfort was that I'd already adjusted to that two-and-a-half-week prison setting in the Federal Detention Center. I knew the inmates, and they knew me. It's very odd that you find comfort in a surrounding that is so foreign. As humans, we often cling to the familiar and resist change. But there is a certain kind of brotherhood among inmates. There's respect for one another. And one thing that I learned very early in this journey, beginning at Three Rivers camp, is that you never look at anyone for very long. You mind your own business.

You respect each other's property. It does not matter what the offenses are, what crime they may have committed, except for child molestation or rape. If there's an inmate who had committed the crime of child molestation or rape, he is immediately moved from the general population, because he is likely to be shanked or beaten. For those who do not know, a shank is the word for a homemade knife made in prison.

It's the strangest setting and hard to describe. Those crimes aside, there is such respect for one another in a prison setting. There is separation. But for some reason, I seemed to get along with all the inmates no matter their ethnicity — black, white, Indian, Asian — we were all equal. We were all men who made poor choices that led to an altering stage in our lives filled with regret, remorse, anger, fear, and solitude.

There's an almost unbearable sense of hopelessness that consumes you when you're in that prison setting. I kept telling myself, "Thank God. I'll be out of here in 16 to 18 months." A lot of the men that I met were there for 10, 20, or 25 years. And there were even several men that were lifers. It's such a horrible setting. While I learned from it, there is no way to sugarcoat the experience. You're reduced to living like an animal. You're told when to wake up and when to go to bed. There is no freedom, only hope and prayers. If it weren't for my connection with God, I don't know how I would have survived. It absolutely got me through that stage.

After being back at the federal prison camp for another week, I then boarded the airplane again, flew to Beaumont, and this time I was escorted to a bus on which I was able to stay and ride to the Beaumont Federal Prison facility. Fear set in again. When we pulled up to Beaumont, there were four prisons sitting on the vast property. There is the Federal Prison Camp, a medium federal prison, then a low federal prison, and a maximum federal prison.

As the bus entered the prison compound, it pulled up to the maximum federal prison first. This is a prison that has guards standing on the tower with shotguns. It is the worst of all prison settings in which to serve a sentence. My heart was pounding fast. Fear set in again — the common theme of my life since everything started falling apart. Like I said, in prison all you have is hope and prayer. So, I turned to God once again, and said, "Oh God, please let them have my paperwork correct. Please don't let them call my name to get off this bus at the maximum federal prison. Thankfully, my name was not called at the maximum prison. I then went to the medium prison. Again, my name was not called when the bus then went to the low prison. At last, we pulled up to the Federal Prison Camp and my name was called. Unlike the other prisons, there is no fence around the camp. It is a series of metal buildings with a baseball field, cafeteria, library, recreation room, and a church. Thank God. My prayers had been answered. My faith had not failed me.

I was now at the Beaumont Camp, where I would serve out my sentence and enter the residential Drug and Alcohol Treatment Program. I can only now look back and truly say what a blessing it was in my life to have gone through this program. I learned so much about myself that I never thought possible. I was so full of fear, not only at the beginning of this prison setting, but fear is what led me to make so many bad decisions in life. I was a people pleaser. I wanted to solve everyone's problems. I wanted to be Robin Hood. I wanted to be liked. I wanted to be loved. I wanted to be respected. I had worked so hard my entire life to build a reputation on trust, honesty, and integrity. I lost all of that by the poor decisions I made. And what I now understand, is that I was led by fear. In the residential Drug and Alcohol Treatment Program, I was taught so much about myself and why I made the choices that I did. I learned that from every choice I made, there was a consequence.

There was a good consequence and a bad consequence. No matter what life holds, we make choices daily. I learned that I don't need to solve problems immediately, that it is okay to ask for help. It is okay to be vulnerable. It's okay to feel uncomfortable with that vulnerability. I was conditioned at an early age. I watched as my dad never asked for help, never showed vulnerability. I thought, as a man and as a father, that I was supposed to handle it all. Fear consumed me. I was never in fear of failure. I was in fear of standing up for myself. Why was it so difficult to say no? I learned in the program that no is the healthiest word in the vocabulary. It is okay to say no. I was so passive.

I acquiesced so much. I gave in. I couldn't say no. Why couldn't I stand up for myself nor stand up for what I truly felt in my heart? I was always trying to please others. And our RDAP taught me that **if you change your thinking, you can change your behavior**. How do I change the patterns that I've been living my whole life? It first starts with honesty.

I had to be honest with myself. I had to take ownership for my actions and understand what it truly meant to say that I accept the consequences for what I had done. I needed to ask for forgiveness. However, I needed to forgive myself first. The hardest part of this journey was admitting that I hurt others with my actions and choices. Half the time when I took the money and committed my crime, I only thought of myself. I kept saying, well, I did it for my family.

If only I would have stopped to say, okay, in taking this money, I'm going to hurt my relationship with my wife, and she will never trust me again. I'll lose my integrity. I'll lose my good reputation. I'll lose my marriage. I'll lose my financial freedom. I'll lose my material possessions. I'll lose the freedom to be free. I could alienate my family, my friends, and my children. I did not imagine nor consider the shame I would bring upon my children, my wife, my family, and partners. I did not think about the things that mattered most. All I thought about was me and resolving the situation that filled me with fear. It was so very selfish. I so much want to be able to talk to Elaine now and tell her how truly sorry I am.

I cannot emphasize it enough — I was so very selfish of the choices I made. I will always be so sorry that I violated Elaine's trust, embarrassed her, humiliated her, and broke her heart. The truth is my marriage was not strong at that time. If I truly had a marriage of strength, my wife would have been the first one I approached to say, "I'm afraid. I don't know what to do. We're going broke. We have lost the three million dollars we had in CDs and cash; every property I have is being foreclosed on. What do I do? I'm afraid." But I was so full of pride. I could not ask for help. I did not feel like I had a strong enough relationship with Elaine to be fully honest, which was so very wrong.

Brené Brown wrote a book and gave a TED talk on vulnerability. I wish I would have read her book and seen the TED talk in 2010, or even before that. I was so caught up in what I thought was success. Doing everything on the surface that appeared to be successful to everyone else. In reality, I wasn't successful at all.

The reality was that I was living in turmoil and conflict with myself every day. I learned in our RDAP program that the greatest part of a foundation begins with honesty, which is what earns trust.

There must be a balance. I was so unbalanced in having a job that's rewarding, while fulfilling a love relationship; community service, physical and mental health relationships with my children and my spouse, communication, the spokes on the wheel were often every spoke in my life. I had three heart attacks. I was not honest with my wife. I was not honest with myself. It was a hard reality to look in the mirror with such disappointment in myself.

But thank God the program that I went through at the camp truly changed my life.

And I'll never be the same. Never, never, never, never be the same. I truly put God first and honesty above all. I go to bed every night and say, "Dear Heavenly Father if I've offended anyone, let me make amends. Dear Heavenly Father, allow me to be the person you created me to be."

Life is a series of unexpected interruptions. And what I choose now is to stand up for myself, not be passive, to say no, and to be proud of my past that I was able to overcome insurmountable odds. But God has given me my best years ahead. It's vital to face your problems today. No matter how big or small. Because today's delay will make tomorrow even tougher.

There is no problem that's too big for God. Know that if you stop, pause, breathe, and ask for help or advice — it is okay. It's not showing you're weak. It's showing you're human. It's showing that you have a heart, and you have feelings — that you're vulnerable and humble.

I always want to remain humble. When I was a millionaire, I was liquid, meaning I had cash in the bank, as well as a net worth of $50 million dollars. I was very confident; I had an ego. Ego and pride can take a man down as it did me. Making money makes one confident, going broke makes one humble. I want to remain confident and humble in all that I do and with every step that I take from this day forward.

It's okay to lose. That's the life lesson. It doesn't matter how many times you lose, it's how many times and how quickly you get back up again. I love dreaming again. I've never felt more confident, because now I know where I'm going. I will not be led by fear. I will not be defined as a felon. I will not look at my past as a detriment, yet as a wonderful life lesson.

I'm so blessed through this journey that I was able to have truly found what true friends are from my family to friends I've known for 25 to 40 years, who stood by my side and are still standing by my side today. The counselors in prison said, "You will lose family members; you will lose friends, but the ones who count will stick with you. They'll never leave you. They'll never judge you. And they'll truly be there to support you and pick you up." I really have a phenomenal support team surrounding me every day of my life. I'm dreaming big again. And I'm living those dreams. I came up with this quote, "Act upon your dreams because the difference in you and those who don't act is the difference in what can become a reality."

I'm living that today.

One thing I learned in RDAP was that a lot of our behavior was really a learned behavior. An example of this is when I was growing up, my father would be home, often in the evening, the phone would ring. That's when we had landlines.

My mother would answer the phone, and the caller would ask, "Is Doug home?" She would say, "No, he's not home. I can take a message," knowing that my dad was right there. Well, at a young age, I couldn't understand why my mother would say my father was not there when he was, so I grew up with these little white lies that seemed like no big deal. Everyone tells a little white lie from time to time. It's okay. I was so embodied in telling the truth all the time. I prided myself that I was honest in everything that I did and that was my whole makeup, and my whole being was that I was honest and respectful. I told the truth. But the little white lies were not telling the truth.

That was just what everyone did, or it's what I thought everyone did. So, when I got to the RDAP program, one of the questions asked was what type of upbringing did you have, what did you have as an influence in your life, who were the people who influenced you, and who are your influences currently? Of course, I referenced it back to my parents. And that's when I looked back and thought, well, I always told the truth except for those little white lies. Well, those little white lies were what added up to me making a series of bad choices, because I didn't look at it as little white lies. I looked at it as it was just not the full truth. But the facts were the facts. Show me a person who tells the truth 95 percent of the time and I'll show you a liar. So, I really was lying to myself, and lying to others as simple as the little white lies.

The RDAP program really made me look at myself and address the things that I never took the time to see that were deep inside. And that program was when it finally hit me that everything was a setup to the bad choices I made. I'm certainly not blaming my parents, I take full responsibility for my actions, but I was always justifying those little white lies.

Another prime example is my younger son often called me to pick him up when he was in high school and not driving yet. He was a freshman in high school and played tennis. He said, "Dad, I need you to pick me up at five o'clock today." And all of a sudden, it's 5:15 p.m., I'm not there yet, and he's calling me. I answered the phone, and he asked, "Dad, where are you?"

I said, "I'm five minutes away." Well, I wasn't really five minutes away. I was 15 to 20 minutes away, but that was always my way of saying I was on my way.

Finally, he said, "Dad, literally, tell me what intersection you are at now, read the signs." When I told him where I was, he said, "Well Dad, you don't have to lie to me. Just tell me you're

20 minutes away." I look back at moments like that, and I think I go back to the little white lies.

Fast forward.

Now I look at what brought me to prison.

And it was all because I was full of fear, I was afraid of telling the truth, and I was afraid of asking for help. I always was the go-to guy. So, everyone came to me to solve their problems, whether it was personal, financial, family, or business partners. So, I solved everyone's problems, but I didn't have anyone to turn to when I had a problem. I kept it all inside.

Another part of the RDAP program was about opening yourself up and asking for help. It's okay to ask for help. As I mentioned before, I was conditioned early on that's not what a man does, it's not what a husband does, it's not what a father does. I'm not going to ask for help. It was a learned behavior; that's what I saw in my dad. My dad never once asked for help. He never showed his vulnerability. He never once, that I know of, turned to my mother or anyone and said, "I'm scared. I'm afraid. What should I do?" That was what I was feeling inside. When I took the money that led me to prison, I was so afraid of not wanting to let anybody know what I was going through, and I didn't want to ask for anyone's help. It's so critical now and I'm grateful for what I learned in the RDAP program.
It's okay to be vulnerable, it's okay to open up your heart. It's okay to ask for help. Those decisions that I could have made back then would have prevented all the heartaches that not only I went through, but also my family, my children, my ex-wife, my business partners, and everybody in my circle.

We're all affected by the choices we make. At the time, I didn't think I was selfish. I thought every choice I made was for my family. I took the money, not to make a car payment, a boat payment, nor a house payment, not anything like that, I took it to pay other real estate debt, and also to pay my ex-wife back on a $500,000 CD that we had cashed in to try and save another shopping center. All the money I took, I immediately gave away. That's called the Robin Hood syndrome, which is what I learned in the RDAP program. The Robin Hood syndrome is where you justify your actions and continue to say, "Oh, I did it for my family." If I *really* had done it for my family, I would never have put them in harm's way nor put them through that humiliation, that heartache, that hurt. It was because I was afraid to tell the truth, ask for help, and show vulnerability.

> *Robin Hood Syndrome. You think you're doing it to help others, when in reality, you're causing more harm than good. I was justifying my poor choices thinking I was doing it all for them. The truth was that I was doing it for me and not thinking of the consequences and the effect my poor choices were having on my family.*
>
> *— Lesson from RDAP*

My last challenge for you is to learn to be comfortable in those uncomfortable situations. Learn to embrace your vulnerability, and not be afraid to ask for help. Even if you are afraid, despite your best efforts, simply reach out to those who have the ability to help, whether by providing emotional support or solutions to your problems. Find ways to be selfless and choose faith over fear. It is my hope that my story inspires and shows you that despite all of life's unexpected interruptions, we must hold onto hope and learn from what seems to be our darkest hours. Let those unexpected interruptions help you shape your future.

Like the Journey song "Don't Stop Believin'."

*"When your dream hits a target
no one else can see,
and your vision hits a target
no one else is pursuing,
you will reach your target.
When execution occurs,
success becomes real.*

Be a doer, not a talker.

*Act upon your dreams
because the difference between
you and those who don't act
is the difference in when
a dream becomes a reality."*

— *Clark East*

About the Author

Clark began his career early, owning a bar/restaurant and limo service at 19 years old. Clark then began his commercial real estate career in 1979 at the age of 22 and then went on to become a successful commercial developer specializing in retail shopping centers spanning Texas, Florida, and North Carolina. Clark developed more than one million square feet of retail space, including not only Shopping centers, but apartments, office buildings, and hotels, exceeding more than $100 million in development. Some of his clients have included Starbucks, CVS, LA Fitness, HomeGoods, GolfSmith, Chipotle, McDonald's, Chili's, Outback Steakhouse, Carrabba's, and Panera Bread.

Always the entrepreneur, Clark founded and was the inventor of the technology and associated device, "TracFind," which tracks anything, anytime, anywhere, and alerts you instantly worldwide. He was awarded his first U.S. Patent in 2015. He also invented the Faith Coin and hands them out on a regular basis to anyone where he feels a connection and needs reassurance.

While originally from Louisiana, Clark's heart is still on the Gulf Coast of Florida, where he grew up. Clark loves boating, the beach, and anything around water. He loves spending time with his four grandkids and his family. Passionate about family, cooking, creating, and giving back.

Follow Clark at:

ClarkEastAuthor.com
Facebook.com/ClarkEastAuthor
Linkedin.com/in/clark-east

www.ingramcontent.com/pod-product-compliance
Lightning Source LLC
Chambersburg PA
CBHW071211070526
44584CB00019B/2992